# CONSTRUCTION SAFETY

*Your Complete Guide to Starting a Career in Safety*

## Sean Amalla, SMP®, CHST®

**FYRE INK Publishing**

Copyright © 2025 Sean Amalla

All rights reserved

The characters and events portrayed in this book are fictitious. Any similarity to real persons, living or dead, is coincidental and not intended by the author.

No part of this book may be reproduced, or stored in a retrieval system, or transmitted in any form or by any means, electronic, mechanical, photocopying, recording, or otherwise, without express written permission of the publisher.

ISBN-13: 9798991070720

Cover design by: Sean Amalla
Printed in the United States of America

*To the mentors who shaped my journey in construction safety: your wisdom, patience, and unwavering belief in me turned challenges into opportunities and lessons into legacy.*

*John Cde Baca, thank you for seeing potential in me long before I did. You taught me to analyze deeply, solve fearlessly, and never settle for "good enough." Your insistence that I present solutions, not just problems, forged the critical thinker I am today.*

*Kenny Herrera, your infectious energy and relentless focus on relationships showed me that leadership is about people, not just policies. You pushed me to think beyond the obvious, fight for what's right (even when it's hard), and trust that influence grows when integrity leads the way.*

*And to my father, Diego Amalla; my first and greatest mentor. You taught me that hard work, honesty, and keeping your word are the foundations of a life well lived. Everything I've accomplished carries the imprint of your values.*

*I love you Dad!*

*To John, Kenny, and Dad:*
*This book exists because of the skills you nurtured, the standards you set, and the faith you never let me lose.*

*With endless love and gratitude - Sean Amalla*

*"In construction safety, every hard hat worn, every harness secured, and every hazard identified is a promise kept; a promise that those who build our world will return home unharmed. This book is for those who seek to dedicate their careers to keeping that promise, one safety measure at a time."*

SEAN AMALLA

# CONTENTS

Title Page
Copyright
Dedication
Epigraph
Foreword

Chapter 1: Understanding the Construction Safety Landscape    1

Chapter 2: Essential Safety Regulations and Standards    14

Chapter 3: The Psychology of Safety    30

Chapter 4: Hazard Recognition and Risk Assessment    48

Chapter 5: Personal Protective Equipment (PPE)    65

Chapter 6: Major Construction Hazards    93

Chapter 7: Educational Pathways and Certifications    122

Chapter 8: Gaining Practical Experience    136

Chapter 9: Essential Skills for Safety Professionals    153

Chapter 10: Developing Effective Safety Programs    168

Chapter 11: Training and Communication    185

Chapter 12: Incident Investigation and Analysis    199

Chapter 13: Safety Management Systems    223

Chapter 14: Emerging Trends and Technologies    239

Chapter 15: Building Your Professional Network    259

Chapter 16: Career Advancement Strategies  282

Chapter 17: Ethical Considerations and Professional Responsibility  293

Appendices  308

# FOREWORD

Construction is more than an industry; it's the backbone of progress. Every hospital, school, bridge, and home begins with the skill and sweat of workers who brave heights, heavy machinery, and unpredictable conditions to turn blueprints into reality. Yet for decades, construction has remained one of America's most dangerous professions. Behind the statistics one in five workplace fatalities are real people: parents, partners, and friends who left for work one morning and never came home.

This book was born from a simple but urgent truth: every one of these tragedies is preventable.

Whether you're a seasoned safety professional, a construction worker transitioning into safety, or a student embarking on this career, you've chosen to stand between hazards and lives. Your role is not just about compliance or checklists; it's about leadership, problem-solving, and fostering a culture where safety is as non-negotiable as quality or schedule.

*Construction Safety: Your Complete Guide to Starting a Career in Safety* distills decades of hard-won knowledge into actionable strategies. You'll learn to:

- **Anticipate hazards** before they turn into incidents, using real-world case studies and risk assessment tools.
- **Communicate effectively** with workers, managers, and

regulators even when faced with skepticism.
- **Leverage technology,** from wearable sensors to BIM, to protect workers in an evolving industry.
- **Build programs** that last, transforming safety from a policy into a shared value.

But this book is not just about what to do. It's about why it matters. The stories of Maria Santos, James Chen, and countless others remind us that safety isn't abstract. It's the difference between a routine day and a life-altering disaster. It's the pride of seeing a project finish on time and with zero injuries. It's the legacy you'll leave in an industry that's safer because you showed up.

To those who've made safety their mission: thank you. The workers on your sites may never know the near-misses you've prevented, but they'll go home because of you. That's the highest achievement any professional can claim.

Now, let's get to work.

**Sean Amalla,** *SMP®, CHST®*
*Co-Founder/COO*
**Contract Safety Professionals, LLC.**

# Preface: Why Construction Safety Matters

Every morning, millions of construction workers across the country put on their hard hats, lace up their boots, and head to job sites where they'll spend their day building the infrastructure that defines our communities. They construct the hospitals where our children are born, the schools where they learn, the bridges we drive across, and the homes where families create memories. These workers are skilled craftspeople, problem solvers, and the backbone of our built environment.

Yet construction remains one of the most dangerous industries in America. According to the Bureau of Labor Statistics, one in five workplace fatalities occurs in construction, despite the industry employing only about 5% of the total workforce. In 2023, 1,056 construction workers died from work-related injuries - that's nearly three deaths every single day. Behind each statistic is a family forever changed, a community that has lost a valued member, and a stark reminder that our work in construction safety isn't just about compliance or regulations - it's about ensuring that every worker who shows up to build our world makes it home safely at the end of the day.

## The Human Cost of Unsafe Practices

Maria Santos was 34 years old when she fell from an improperly secured scaffold on a residential construction project in Phoenix. She left behind two young children and a husband who still struggles to explain to their six-year-old why mommy isn't coming home. James Chen, a 28-year-old electrician, was electrocuted when proper lockout procedures weren't followed during maintenance work on a commercial building in Seattle. His parents had immigrated to give him opportunities they never had, and he was just three months away from starting his own electrical contracting business.

These aren't isolated incidents. They represent a systemic challenge that has persisted in our industry for decades. The difference between a safe job site and a dangerous one often comes down to one factor: the presence of knowledgeable, dedicated safety professionals who understand that their role extends far beyond checking boxes on compliance forms.

## The Economic Reality

While the human cost of construction accidents is immeasurable, the economic impact is staggering. Workplace injuries and illnesses in construction cost employers more than $13 billion annually in direct costs alone. When you factor in indirect costs - lost productivity, training replacement workers, schedule delays, legal fees, and increased insurance premiums - the total economic impact can be four to six times higher.

Consider the ripple effects of a single serious incident: A crane collapse on a high-rise project doesn't just injure workers; it can shut down an entire job site for weeks or months, delay occupancy for tenants, impact dozens of subcontractors, and result in millions of dollars in costs that ultimately affect everyone from property owners to the communities waiting for new housing or commercial space.

Smart business leaders have learned that investing in comprehensive safety programs isn't just the right thing to do - it's the profitable thing to do. Companies with strong safety cultures consistently report lower insurance costs, reduced turnover, improved productivity, and better relationships with clients who increasingly demand safety excellence from their contractors.

## Your Role in Transforming an Industry

This is where you come in. Whether you're a recent graduate considering a career in construction safety, an experienced construction professional looking to transition into safety, or someone who has always been passionate about protecting workers, you have the opportunity to be part of the solution.

Construction safety professionals are the guardians of worker welfare. You'll be the person who identifies hazards before they cause harm, who develops training programs that save lives, who investigates incidents to prevent their recurrence, and who advocates for the resources and attention that safety deserves on every project. You'll work with everyone from entry-level laborers to C-suite executives, translating complex regulations into practical solutions that work in the real world.

The construction industry is experiencing unprecedented change. New technologies are revolutionizing how we build, from prefabrication and modular construction to robotics and artificial intelligence. Demographic shifts are bringing more diversity to construction workforces, requiring safety professionals who can communicate across language and cultural barriers. Climate change is creating new hazards and working conditions that didn't exist a generation ago.

These changes create both challenges and opportunities for safety professionals. The companies and projects that thrive in this evolving landscape will be those that prioritize worker safety and have skilled professionals who can navigate complexity while keeping people safe.

## What This Book Will Do for You

This book is designed to be your comprehensive guide for launching and building a successful career in construction safety. Unlike academic textbooks that focus purely on theory or technical manuals that dive deep into specific regulations, this book bridges the gap between knowledge and practice. You'll learn not just what you need to know, but how to apply that knowledge effectively in real-world situations.

We'll start with the foundational knowledge every safety professional needs: understanding the regulatory landscape, recognizing hazards, and grasping the human factors that influence safety behavior. Then we'll dive into the technical skills that will make you effective: conducting risk assessments, developing safety programs, investigating incidents, and training workers.

But technical knowledge alone isn't enough. You'll also learn the soft skills that separate good safety professionals from great ones: how to communicate persuasively with skeptical supervisors, how to influence behavior when you don't have direct authority, how to build trust with workers who may be suspicious of "safety people," and how to navigate the political realities of construction projects where schedule and budget pressures can create conflicts with safety priorities.

Throughout the book, you'll find real-world case studies that illustrate both failures and successes, practical tools you can use immediately, and insights from experienced professionals who have built successful careers in construction safety. You'll learn about different career paths within the field, from corporate safety management to consulting, from regulatory work to specialized areas like industrial hygiene or ergonomics.

## A Personal Mission

Every safety professional has a moment when the importance of their work becomes crystal clear. For some, it's preventing their first serious accident through early hazard recognition. For others, it's investigating an incident and realizing how easily it could have been prevented with better procedures. For many, it's simply the daily satisfaction of knowing that families are reunited each evening because of their diligent work.

Your journey in construction safety isn't just about building a career - it's about joining a mission to transform an industry. Every hazard you identify, every training session you deliver, every safety culture improvement you implement has the potential to prevent injuries, save lives, and help construction workers return home safely to their families.

The construction industry needs more dedicated, well-trained safety professionals. Workers deserve advocates who understand both the technical aspects of safety and the practical realities of construction work. Companies need professionals who can help them achieve their safety goals while maintaining productivity and profitability.

As you begin this journey, remember that you're not just learning about construction safety - you're preparing to become a guardian of worker welfare, a champion for safety culture, and a professional who can make a meaningful difference in one of America's most essential industries.

The workers building our future are counting on professionals like you to keep them safe. Let's make sure you're ready for that responsibility.

# Construction Safety:
## Your Complete Guide to Starting a Career in Safety

# CHAPTER 1: UNDERSTANDING THE CONSTRUCTION SAFETY LANDSCAPE

Construction sites are dynamic environments where progress is measured in concrete poured, steel erected, and systems installed. Yet beneath this visible progress lies an invisible network of hazards that can turn routine tasks into life-threatening situations in seconds. Understanding the current state of construction safety - its challenges, improvements, and ongoing evolution - is essential for anyone entering this critical field.

## The Numbers Tell a Story

The statistics surrounding construction safety paint a picture that is both sobering and motivating. While construction represents approximately 5% of the total U.S. workforce, it accounts for nearly 20% of all workplace fatalities. In 2023, the construction industry recorded 1,056 worker deaths, maintaining its position as the industry with the most workplace fatalities for the thirteenth consecutive year.

These numbers represent more than statistical data - they reflect real families, real communities, and real opportunities for improvement. The construction fatality rate of 9.6 deaths per 100,000 full-time equivalent workers is nearly three times higher than the all-industry average of 3.7. However, these figures also tell a story of progress. In 1970, when the Occupational Safety and Health Administration (OSHA) was created, construction fatality rates were more than five times higher than today's levels.

This improvement didn't happen by accident. It resulted from dedicated safety professionals, regulatory enforcement, technological advances, and a gradual shift in industry culture that increasingly values worker protection alongside productivity and profitability.

**Regional and Sector Variations**
Construction safety challenges aren't uniform across the country or across different types of construction work. States with rapid population growth and extensive construction activity, such as Texas, Florida, and California, consistently report the highest absolute numbers of construction fatalities. However, when adjusted for the size of the construction workforce, rural states often show higher fatality rates, potentially reflecting differences in regulatory oversight, available safety resources, and project complexity.

Different construction sectors also present varying risk profiles. Heavy and civil engineering construction, which includes highway, bridge, and utility work, has historically shown higher fatality rates than building construction. Specialty trade contractors, particularly those working in roofing, electrical, and excavation, face specific hazards that require targeted safety approaches.

# The Fatal Four: Understanding Primary Hazards

OSHA has identified four hazard categories that account for more than half of all construction fatalities. Understanding these "Fatal Four" provides insight into where safety professionals can have the greatest impact.

## Falls

Falls represent the leading cause of construction fatalities, accounting for approximately 36% of all deaths in the industry. These incidents occur across all construction sectors and affect workers at every experience level. Falls from roofs, scaffolds, ladders, and elevated work platforms continue to claim lives despite decades of safety improvements and regulatory attention.

The complexity of fall protection lies not just in the variety of potential fall hazards, but in the dynamic nature of construction work. Unlike manufacturing environments where hazards remain relatively constant, construction sites change daily. Today's safe walking surface becomes tomorrow's fall hazard as work progresses and new elevations are created.

Modern fall protection has evolved far beyond simple safety harnesses. Today's systems include engineered fall protection plans, passive protection systems like guardrails and safety nets, and advanced personal fall arrest systems with shock-absorbing lanyards and self-retracting lifelines. However, the most sophisticated equipment is only effective when workers are properly trained, equipment is regularly inspected, and site conditions are continuously evaluated.

## Struck-by Objects

The second leading cause of construction fatalities involves workers being struck by falling, flying, swinging, or rolling objects. These incidents can occur when cranes drop loads, when tools fall from elevated work areas, when vehicles strike workers, or when materials are improperly stored or handled. Struck-by incidents often result from breakdowns in communication and coordination. A crane operator may not see a worker in the swing radius. A truck driver backing up may not notice a worker behind the vehicle. Materials stacked improperly may fall when vibrations from nearby work destabilize the pile.

Preventing struck-by incidents requires comprehensive hazard recognition, clear communication protocols, proper personal protective equipment, and systematic approaches to material handling and storage. Technology increasingly plays a role, with proximity sensors, backup alarms, and spotting systems helping to prevent these tragic incidents.

## Electrocution

Electrical hazards cause approximately 8% of construction fatalities, but their impact extends beyond these numbers. Electrical incidents often result in severe burns, permanent disabilities, and secondary injuries from falls or other reactions to electrical shock. Construction electrical hazards differ significantly from those in industrial settings because construction often involves work near overhead power lines, temporary electrical systems, and equipment operating in harsh outdoor conditions.

The complexity of construction electrical safety lies in the interaction between permanent electrical systems and temporary construction power. Workers may encounter energized circuits they didn't expect, use damaged extension cords, or work with wet conditions that increase electrical risks. Additionally, construction work frequently occurs near overhead power lines, creating hazards for crane operators, workers on elevated platforms, and anyone handling conductive materials.

**Caught-in/Between**
The fourth category of the Fatal Four involves workers being caught in or compressed by equipment, objects, or collapsing structures. Trenching and excavation work represents a significant portion of these incidents, as cave-ins can trap workers with little warning. Other caught-in/between incidents involve workers being caught in machinery, compressed between vehicles and fixed objects, or trapped in confined spaces.

Excavation-related fatalities are particularly tragic because they are highly preventable through proper protective systems. Trenches deeper than five feet require protective systems such as sloping, shoring, or trench boxes. However, economic pressures, tight schedules, and inadequate training sometimes lead to shortcuts that cost lives.

# Beyond the Fatal Four: Emerging Hazards

While the Fatal Four represent the most common causes of construction fatalities, safety professionals must also understand emerging and evolving hazards that affect worker health and safety.

**Heat-Related Illness**
Climate change and increasing summer temperatures have made heat-related illness a growing concern in construction. Outdoor construction work often occurs during the hottest parts of the day, with workers wearing heavy clothing and

using physically demanding tools. Heat exhaustion, heat stroke, and related conditions can develop quickly, particularly among workers who are not acclimated to hot conditions or who have underlying health conditions.

Preventing heat-related illness requires proactive planning, including scheduling work during cooler parts of the day, providing adequate hydration and cooling areas, implementing work-rest cycles, and training supervisors to recognize early signs of heat stress.

**Chemical Exposures**
Modern construction involves an increasing array of chemical products, from advanced adhesives and sealants to engineered materials that may release harmful substances during cutting or installation. Silica exposure from cutting concrete, masonry, and stone has received increased regulatory attention as the link between silica dust and serious lung diseases has become clearer.

Chemical hazard management in construction is complicated by the temporary nature of most construction work, the variety of products used, and the challenges of implementing engineering controls in outdoor, changing environments. Safety professionals must stay current with evolving chemical hazards and help develop practical approaches to exposure control.

**Ergonomic Hazards**
The physical demands of construction work contribute to high rates of musculoskeletal disorders, including back injuries, shoulder problems, and knee issues. While these injuries may not result in immediate fatalities, they can end careers, cause long-term disability, and significantly impact workers' quality of life.

Addressing ergonomic hazards in construction requires understanding both the physical demands of specific tasks and the individual factors that influence injury risk. Solutions may include mechanical lifting aids, ergonomic tools, job rotation, and training in proper lifting and material handling techniques.

## The Evolution of Safety Culture

Understanding today's construction safety landscape requires appreciating how safety culture has evolved over the past several decades. The transformation from viewing safety as an individual responsibility to recognizing it as a management system represents one of the most significant changes in construction safety thinking.

### From Blame to System Thinking

Historically, construction accidents were often attributed to worker carelessness or failure to follow safety rules. This approach, while containing elements of truth, failed to address the underlying system factors that contributed to incidents. Modern safety thinking recognizes that accidents typically result from multiple contributing factors, including inadequate training, poor communication, time pressures, inadequate equipment, and organizational factors.

This shift toward systems thinking has profound implications for safety professionals. Rather than simply enforcing rules and investigating accidents to assign blame, today's safety professionals must understand and address the complex interactions between people, equipment, procedures, and organizational factors that influence safety performance.

### The Role of Leadership

Research has consistently shown that visible, committed leadership is the single most important factor in achieving excellent safety performance. Construction companies with strong safety records invariably have leaders who demonstrate their commitment to safety through their actions, not just their words.

Effective safety leadership in construction involves several key elements: setting clear expectations for safety performance, providing adequate resources for safety programs, holding managers accountable for safety outcomes, and consistently prioritizing safety when it conflicts with other business objectives. Leaders who cut safety corners during busy periods or fail to support safety professionals when difficult decisions must be made undermine their entire safety program.

**Worker Engagement and Empowerment**
Modern safety culture recognizes that workers closest to the hazards often have the best insights into practical solutions. Effective safety programs actively engage workers in hazard identification, solution development, and program improvement. This engagement goes beyond traditional safety committees to include regular job hazard analyses, near-miss reporting systems, and recognition programs that reward proactive safety behavior.

Worker empowerment also includes the right and responsibility to stop work when unsafe conditions exist. Creating an environment where workers feel comfortable exercising stop-work authority requires trust, training, and consistent management support for workers who identify safety concerns.

# Regulatory Framework and Its Impact

The regulatory landscape significantly influences construction safety practices. Understanding this framework helps safety professionals navigate compliance requirements while developing programs that go beyond minimum regulatory standards.

## OSHA's Construction Standards

The Occupational Safety and Health Administration's construction standards, found in 29 CFR Part 1926, provide the primary regulatory framework for construction safety in the United States. These standards address everything from personal protective equipment and fall protection to excavation safety and crane operations.

OSHA's approach to construction safety has evolved from prescriptive standards that specify exactly what must be done to performance-based standards that specify outcomes while allowing flexibility in methods. This evolution reflects recognition that construction work is too varied and dynamic for purely prescriptive approaches to be effective.

Understanding OSHA standards requires more than memorizing specific requirements. Safety professionals must understand the intent behind standards, stay current with regulatory interpretations and enforcement guidance, and help their organizations develop practical approaches to compliance that enhance rather than hinder productivity.

## State and Local Variations

While OSHA provides federal minimum standards, many states operate their own occupational safety and health programs under OSHA oversight. These state programs must be at least as effective as federal OSHA, but they can implement more stringent requirements. Some states have developed construction-specific regulations that exceed federal requirements, particularly in areas such as trench safety, crane operations, and fall protection.

Local jurisdictions may also impose safety requirements through building codes, permit conditions, or local ordinances. Safety professionals must understand the regulatory requirements that apply to their specific projects and locations.

### International Perspectives
As construction companies increasingly work on international projects, understanding global approaches to construction safety becomes important. Countries such as the United Kingdom, Australia, and several European nations have implemented construction safety regulations that differ from U.S. approaches, sometimes providing insights into alternative methods for achieving safety objectives.

These international perspectives can inform domestic safety practices, particularly in areas such as design for safety, worker consultation requirements, and performance-based regulatory approaches.

## Technology's Transformative Impact
The construction industry is experiencing rapid technological change that is transforming both construction methods and safety practices. Understanding these technological trends is essential for safety professionals who want to remain effective in an evolving industry.

### Digital Safety Tools
Smartphones, tablets, and cloud-based software are revolutionizing how safety professionals collect information,

conduct inspections, and manage safety programs. Mobile apps allow real-time hazard reporting, digital forms streamline inspection processes, and data analytics help identify trends and patterns that weren't previously visible.

Wearable technology, including smart hard hats, safety vests with built-in sensors, and personal air quality monitors, provides real-time information about worker exposure to hazards. These devices can alert workers to dangerous conditions and provide safety professionals with data to improve hazard controls.

## Building Information Modeling (BIM) and Safety

Building Information Modeling technology allows safety professionals to identify potential hazards during the design phase, before construction begins. BIM models can simulate construction sequences, identify fall hazards, plan temporary protective systems, and optimize material storage and movement to reduce struck-by hazards.

This proactive approach to hazard identification represents a significant advance over traditional approaches that address hazards only after they appear on job sites. Safety professionals who understand BIM technology can have much greater impact on project safety outcomes.

## Automation and Robotics

Increasing automation in construction, from autonomous vehicles and robotic equipment to prefabricated building systems, is changing the nature of construction hazards. While automation can eliminate some traditional hazards, it also creates new risks related to human-machine interaction, maintenance of complex systems, and the need for specialized training.

Safety professionals must understand these evolving technologies to develop appropriate safety procedures and training programs for workers who will interact with automated systems.

## Looking Forward: Your Role in the Evolving Landscape

The construction safety landscape you're entering is dynamic, challenging, and full of opportunities to make a meaningful difference. The statistics we've discussed represent not just numbers, but opportunities for improvement. The hazards we've identified are problems waiting for solutions. The cultural evolution we've described creates openings for safety professionals who can bridge traditional construction culture with modern safety thinking.

Your success as a construction safety professional will depend on your ability to understand this complex landscape while maintaining focus on the fundamental goal: ensuring that every construction worker returns home safely at the end of each workday. The technical knowledge, regulatory understanding, and cultural awareness you develop will serve as tools to achieve this goal, but your dedication to worker welfare will provide the motivation to use these tools effectively.

The construction industry needs safety professionals who can navigate regulatory complexity while developing practical solutions, who can leverage new technologies while maintaining focus on fundamental hazard controls, and who can work within existing organizational cultures while advocating for continuous improvement. The following chapters will provide you with the knowledge and skills needed to meet these challenges and build a successful career in construction safety.

As you begin this journey, remember that every hazard you identify, every worker you train, and every incident you prevent contributes to the ongoing transformation of construction safety culture. The industry's future depends on professionals like you who are committed to making construction work safer for everyone.

# CHAPTER 2: ESSENTIAL SAFETY REGULATIONS AND STANDARDS

Walking onto any construction site in America, you'll encounter the visible results of decades of regulatory development: workers wearing hard hats and safety glasses, guardrails protecting elevated work areas, warning signs marking hazardous zones, and safety data sheets posted near chemical storage areas. These familiar safety features exist because of a complex web of regulations, standards, and industry practices that have evolved to protect construction workers.

Understanding this regulatory landscape is fundamental to your success as a construction safety professional. You'll need to navigate federal OSHA standards, state regulations, local building codes, and industry consensus standards while helping your organization develop practical approaches to compliance that enhance rather than hinder productivity. This chapter provides you with the knowledge you need to understand, interpret, and apply the regulations that govern construction safety.

# The Foundation: OSHA Construction Standards

The Occupational Safety and Health Administration's construction standards, codified in 29 CFR Part 1926, form the backbone of construction safety regulation in the United States. These standards were developed through a complex process involving industry input, scientific research, and years of practical experience with what works - and what doesn't - in construction safety.

### Understanding OSHA's Structure and Approach

OSHA operates under the principle that employers have a fundamental responsibility to provide a workplace "free from recognized hazards." This concept, embodied in Section 5(a)(1) of the OSH Act and known as the General Duty Clause, extends beyond specific regulatory requirements to encompass any hazard that could reasonably be expected to cause death or serious physical harm.

The construction standards are organized into subparts that address different aspects of construction work. Understanding this organization helps you navigate the regulations more effectively and ensures you don't overlook relevant requirements when addressing specific hazards.

**Subpart C - General Safety and Health Provisions** establishes fundamental requirements that apply across all construction activities. This includes the requirement for competent persons, safety training programs, and basic safety and health provisions that form the foundation for all other construction safety efforts.

**Subpart D - Occupational Health and Environmental Controls** addresses health hazards including noise exposure, respiratory protection, and hazardous materials. This subpart is particularly important as construction work increasingly involves exposure to chemical hazards that may not cause immediate injury but can result in serious long-term health effects.

**Subpart E - Personal Protective and Life Saving Equipment** covers the selection, use, and maintenance of personal protective equipment. While PPE represents the last line of defense in the hierarchy of controls, understanding these requirements is essential because construction work often involves situations where other control methods aren't feasible.

**Subpart F - Fire Protection and Prevention** establishes requirements for fire safety during construction, including provisions for fire extinguishers, emergency procedures, and hot work permits. Construction sites present unique fire hazards due to temporary electrical systems, flammable materials, and hot work activities.

## Critical Construction Standards

Several OSHA construction standards deserve special attention because they address the most common and serious hazards in construction work.

### Fall Protection (Subpart M)

The fall protection standard represents one of OSHA's most comprehensive and frequently cited construction regulations. The standard requires fall protection when workers are exposed to falls of six feet or more, but this simple statement conceals significant complexity in implementation.

The standard establishes a hierarchy of fall protection methods, preferencing passive systems that don't require individual worker action over personal fall arrest systems that depend on proper use by individual workers. Guardrail systems, safety net systems, and personal fall arrest systems each have specific design and performance requirements that must be met to ensure worker protection.

Understanding fall protection requirements involves more than memorizing the six-foot trigger height. You must understand when different types of protection are required, how to evaluate the adequacy of existing protection systems, and how to develop fall protection plans for complex construction situations. The standard also includes specific requirements for different types of construction work, from residential construction to steel erection, reflecting the diverse nature of fall hazards across construction sectors.

**Excavation and Trenching (Subpart P)**
Excavation work presents some of the most serious hazards in construction, with cave-ins capable of trapping and killing workers in seconds. The excavation standard requires protective systems for trenches and excavations deeper than five feet, but like fall protection, this simple requirement involves complex implementation decisions.

The standard allows several methods for protecting workers in excavations: sloping the sides to stable angles, installing shoring systems to prevent cave-ins, or using trench boxes that protect workers even if cave-ins occur. Each method has specific design requirements and limitations that must be understood to ensure adequate protection.

Competent person requirements are particularly important in excavation work. The standard requires that a competent person classify soil conditions, design protective systems, and conduct daily inspections of excavations. This person must have specific training and experience that enables them to identify hazards and authorize appropriate protective measures.

**Scaffolding (Subpart L)**
Scaffolding provides temporary work platforms for construction activities, but it also creates significant fall and structural collapse hazards if not properly designed, erected, and maintained. The scaffolding standard includes detailed requirements for different types of scaffolding systems, from simple tube and coupler scaffolds to complex suspended scaffolds.

The standard establishes requirements for scaffold design, including load capacity, structural integrity, and fall protection systems. It also requires that scaffolds be erected, altered, and dismantled under the supervision of competent persons who understand the specific requirements for the type of scaffold being used.

Platform requirements, access requirements, and fall protection requirements for scaffolds involve complex interactions between different parts of the standard. Safety professionals must understand these interactions to ensure that scaffold systems provide adequate protection for workers.

**Crane and Rigging Operations (Subpart CC)**
Crane operations present multiple serious hazards, including struck-by hazards from falling loads, electrocution from contact with power lines, and structural collapse from crane instability or overloading. The crane standard, which was significantly revised in 2010, establishes comprehensive requirements for crane operations, operator qualification, and rigging activities.

The standard requires that cranes be inspected before each use, that operators be qualified for the specific equipment they operate, and that lifting operations be planned and supervised by qualified persons. It also establishes requirements for working near power lines, load handling, and crane assembly and disassembly.

Understanding crane safety requirements involves both the specific regulatory requirements and the industry standards that are incorporated by reference. The standard references numerous consensus standards developed by organizations such as the American Society of Mechanical Engineers (ASME) and the American National Standards Institute (ANSI).

## State OSHA Programs: Variations and Enhancements

Twenty-two states and territories operate their own occupational safety and health programs under OSHA oversight. These state programs must be "at least as effective" as federal OSHA, but they can implement more stringent requirements and may have different enforcement priorities and procedures.

### Understanding State Program Differences

State OSHA programs often reflect regional construction practices, local hazards, and state-specific priorities. For example, states with significant earthquake risks may have enhanced requirements for temporary structures and fall protection during seismic events. States with extreme weather conditions may have specific requirements for heat illness prevention or cold weather protection.

Some state programs have developed construction-specific regulations that exceed federal requirements. California's construction safety orders include more stringent fall protection requirements, specific heat illness prevention standards, and enhanced requirements for trenching and excavation work. These state-specific requirements can significantly impact how construction projects are planned and executed.

**Enforcement Variations**
State OSHA programs may have different enforcement philosophies and procedures than federal OSHA. Some states emphasize consultation and voluntary compliance programs, while others focus on traditional enforcement activities. Understanding the enforcement approach in your jurisdiction helps you develop appropriate compliance strategies and maintain effective relationships with regulatory agencies.

State programs may also have different penalty structures, citation procedures, and appeal processes. Safety professionals working in state program jurisdictions need to understand these differences to effectively represent their organizations in regulatory interactions.

# Local Building Codes and Ordinances
Local jurisdictions often impose safety requirements through building codes, permit conditions, and local ordinances. These requirements can supplement or exceed federal and state OSHA standards, creating additional compliance obligations for construction projects.

**Building Code Safety Provisions**
Model building codes such as the International Building Code (IBC) include provisions that affect construction safety, particularly during demolition work, structural

modifications, and work in occupied buildings. These provisions may require specific safety measures, notification procedures, or protective systems that aren't addressed in OSHA standards.

Local building codes may also include provisions for construction site security, noise control, and environmental protection that indirectly affect worker safety. Understanding these requirements helps you develop comprehensive safety programs that address all applicable regulations.

**Municipal Safety Ordinances**
Many cities and counties have adopted local ordinances that address construction safety issues. These ordinances may establish requirements for crane operations, trenching permits, hot work permits, or construction site safety measures. Some jurisdictions require specific safety training for workers or mandate the presence of safety professionals on certain types of projects.

Local ordinances may also establish procedures for reporting accidents, investigating incidents, or coordinating with emergency services. Understanding these local requirements is essential for maintaining compliance and ensuring effective emergency response capabilities.

## Industry Consensus Standards

While OSHA standards provide minimum legal requirements, industry consensus standards often provide more detailed guidance on achieving safe working conditions. These standards, developed by organizations such as ANSI, ASME, and the National Fire Protection Association (NFPA), represent the collective expertise of industry professionals and are often incorporated by reference in OSHA standards.

## American National Standards Institute (ANSI)

ANSI coordinates the development of voluntary consensus standards across many industries, including construction. ANSI standards relevant to construction safety include requirements for personal protective equipment, fall protection systems, scaffolding, and construction equipment.

ANSI Z359 standards address fall protection systems and provide detailed requirements for the design, testing, and use of fall protection equipment. These standards are often more detailed than OSHA requirements and provide valuable guidance for developing comprehensive fall protection programs.

ANSI Z87.1 establishes requirements for occupational eye and face protection, including specific requirements for construction environments. Understanding these standards helps you select appropriate eye protection for different construction hazards and ensure that protective equipment meets performance requirements.

## American Society of Mechanical Engineers (ASME)

ASME develops standards for mechanical equipment, including construction equipment such as cranes, hoists, and excavators. ASME B30 standards provide comprehensive requirements for the construction, installation, operation, inspection, and maintenance of lifting equipment.

These standards are incorporated by reference in OSHA's crane standard and provide detailed guidance on safe crane operations. Understanding ASME standards is essential for anyone involved in crane safety, rigging operations, or heavy equipment management.

## National Fire Protection Association (NFPA)

NFPA develops standards for fire safety, including standards that are particularly relevant to construction work. NFPA 241 addresses safeguarding construction, alteration, and demolition operations from fire hazards, while NFPA 51B provides requirements for fire prevention during cutting and welding operations.

These standards provide detailed guidance on fire prevention measures, hot work permits, fire watch procedures, and emergency response planning for construction sites. Understanding NFPA standards helps you develop comprehensive fire safety programs that protect both workers and property.

# International Standards and Their Influence

As construction companies increasingly work on international projects, understanding global approaches to construction safety becomes important. International standards organizations such as the International Organization for Standardization (ISO) have developed safety management standards that are being adopted by construction companies worldwide.

### ISO 45001: Occupational Health and Safety Management Systems

ISO 45001 provides a framework for occupational health and safety management systems that can be applied to construction organizations. This standard emphasizes risk-based thinking, worker participation, and continuous improvement in safety performance.

While ISO 45001 doesn't establish specific technical requirements like OSHA standards, it provides a systematic approach to managing safety that can enhance compliance with regulatory requirements. Understanding this standard helps you develop comprehensive safety management systems that go beyond minimum regulatory compliance.

### International Perspectives on Construction Safety

Other countries have developed construction safety regulations that differ from U.S. approaches and may provide insights into alternative methods for achieving safety objectives. The United Kingdom's Construction (Design and Management) Regulations place significant emphasis on designing out hazards during the planning phase, while Australia's work health and safety laws establish comprehensive consultation requirements with workers.

These international approaches can inform domestic safety practices and provide ideas for enhancing existing safety programs. Understanding global best practices helps you develop more effective approaches to construction safety challenges.

## Practical Application: Developing Compliance Strategies

Understanding regulations is only the first step in effective safety management. You must also develop practical approaches to compliance that work within the constraints of construction projects while achieving the safety objectives that regulations are designed to accomplish.

### Risk-Based Compliance Approaches

Rather than attempting to address every possible regulatory requirement with equal emphasis, effective safety professionals develop risk-based approaches that focus resources on the most significant hazards and compliance issues. This involves understanding which regulations apply to specific work activities, which violations are most likely to result in serious injuries, and which regulatory issues are most likely to result in enforcement actions.

Risk-based compliance involves conducting regular assessments of regulatory requirements, identifying areas where current practices may not meet regulatory standards, and developing corrective action plans that address the most significant risks first.

**Integration with Project Management**
Regulatory compliance must be integrated with overall project management processes to be effective. This means understanding how regulatory requirements affect project scheduling, resource allocation, and coordination between different trades and contractors.

Effective integration involves developing project-specific safety plans that address applicable regulations, establishing procedures for ensuring compliance throughout the project lifecycle, and creating accountability systems that ensure regulatory requirements are consistently met.

**Training and Communication**
Regulatory compliance depends on workers and supervisors understanding and implementing regulatory requirements in their daily work activities. This requires ongoing training programs that translate regulatory requirements into practical work procedures and effective communication systems that keep everyone informed about regulatory requirements and changes.

Training programs must address both the specific requirements of applicable regulations and the practical skills needed to implement those requirements safely and efficiently. Communication systems must ensure that regulatory information reaches the right people at the right time to influence their work activities.

## Staying Current with Regulatory Changes

Construction safety regulations continue to evolve as new hazards are identified, new technologies are developed, and enforcement experience reveals areas where existing regulations need improvement. Staying current with these changes is essential for maintaining compliance and ensuring that your safety programs remain effective.

### OSHA's Regulatory Development Process

Understanding how OSHA develops new regulations helps you anticipate future requirements and participate in the regulatory development process. OSHA typically issues advance notices of proposed rulemaking, requests for information, and proposed rules before finalizing new regulations. Participating in these processes allows you to influence regulatory development and prepare your organization for new requirements.

OSHA also issues interpretation letters, compliance directives, and enforcement guidance that clarify how existing regulations will be applied. Staying current with these documents helps you understand evolving enforcement priorities and compliance expectations.

### Professional Development and Networking

Professional organizations, industry associations, and educational institutions provide valuable resources for staying current with regulatory changes. Professional conferences, webinars, and training programs often feature presentations on new regulations and enforcement trends.

Networking with other safety professionals, regulatory officials, and industry experts provides insights into practical compliance approaches and emerging regulatory issues. These relationships can be invaluable for understanding how regulations are being interpreted and applied in practice.

## Building Your Regulatory Expertise

Developing expertise in construction safety regulations requires more than reading the standards and attending training programs. You must develop practical skills in interpreting regulations, applying them to specific situations, and helping others understand their compliance obligations.

### Interpretation Skills

Regulatory interpretation involves understanding both the specific language of regulations and their underlying intent. This requires understanding the regulatory development process, the hazards that regulations are designed to address, and the practical constraints that affect implementation.

Effective interpretation also involves understanding how different regulations interact with each other and how they apply to specific construction activities. This systems approach to regulatory interpretation helps you develop comprehensive compliance strategies that address all applicable requirements.

### Application Skills

Applying regulations to specific construction situations requires understanding both the regulatory requirements and the practical aspects of construction work. This involves site visits, discussions with workers and supervisors, and hands-on experience with construction activities.

Effective application also requires understanding the economic and operational constraints that affect compliance decisions. The most technically correct regulatory interpretation may not be practical if it significantly increases costs or delays project completion.

**Teaching and Communication Skills**
Much of your work as a safety professional will involve helping others understand and implement regulatory requirements. This requires developing skills in training design, presentation, and communication that enable you to translate complex regulatory requirements into practical guidance.

Effective teaching also involves understanding different learning styles, cultural differences, and the practical constraints that affect how people learn and apply new information. These skills are essential for developing training programs that actually change behavior and improve compliance.

# Your Role in the Regulatory Landscape
As a construction safety professional, you serve as a bridge between the regulatory world and the practical world of construction work. Your success depends on your ability to understand regulatory requirements, interpret them correctly, and help others implement them effectively.

This role involves more than enforcement or compliance checking. You must also serve as an advocate for practical regulatory approaches, a source of expertise for complex compliance questions, and a catalyst for continuous improvement in safety performance.

The regulatory landscape will continue to evolve throughout your career, presenting both challenges and opportunities. New hazards will emerge, new technologies will be developed, and new approaches to safety management will be proven effective. Your ability to adapt to these changes while maintaining focus on fundamental safety principles will determine your long-term success as a construction safety professional.

Understanding regulations provides the foundation for your professional practice, but it's only the beginning. The following chapters will build on this regulatory foundation to help you develop the technical skills, practical experience, and professional judgment needed to excel in construction safety. Remember that regulations establish minimum requirements - your goal is to help your organization achieve safety performance that exceeds these minimums and truly protects workers from the hazards they face every day.

# CHAPTER 3: THE PSYCHOLOGY OF SAFETY

On a busy construction site in Denver, two experienced carpenters are installing floor joists on the second story of a residential project. Both workers have received identical safety training, use the same equipment, and work under the same supervisor. The safety regulations are clear: fall protection is required when working at heights above six feet. Personal fall arrest equipment is readily available. Yet one worker consistently uses his safety harness while the other finds reasons to work without protection - "just for a few minutes" or "just this once."

This scenario plays out on construction sites every day and illustrates a fundamental truth about construction safety: human behavior, not just technical knowledge or regulatory compliance, ultimately determines whether workers go home safely. Understanding the psychological factors that influence safety behavior is essential for any construction safety professional who wants to move beyond checking boxes to actually preventing injuries.

The psychology of safety encompasses how people perceive

risk, make decisions under pressure, respond to social influences, and adapt their behavior based on experience and consequences. These psychological principles apply to everyone on construction sites, from entry-level workers to senior executives, and understanding them will make you more effective at creating lasting safety improvements.

## Understanding Human Risk Perception

Humans are remarkably poor at accurately assessing risks, particularly the types of low-probability, high-consequence events that characterize many construction accidents. Our brains evolved to help our ancestors survive immediate physical threats like predators or natural disasters, not to evaluate the statistical likelihood of industrial accidents or long-term health effects from chemical exposures.

### The Optimism Bias

Most people believe they are less likely than others to experience negative events - a phenomenon psychologists call optimism bias. Construction workers often acknowledge that accidents happen in their industry while simultaneously believing that accidents won't happen to them personally. This bias can lead to risk-taking behavior because workers underestimate their personal vulnerability to hazards.

Understanding optimism bias helps explain why generic safety statistics often fail to motivate behavior change. Telling workers that "construction workers are injured at high rates" may not resonate because each individual worker believes he or she is different from the statistics. More effective approaches focus on specific, immediate risks and help workers understand how their personal actions directly influence their safety outcomes.

## Availability Heuristic

People tend to judge the likelihood of events based on how easily they can remember similar events - a mental shortcut called the availability heuristic. Workers who have recently witnessed or heard about accidents tend to be more safety-conscious, while those who haven't experienced accidents may underestimate risks.

This principle explains why safety performance often improves temporarily after serious accidents but gradually declines as memories fade. Effective safety programs must find ways to keep safety concerns "available" in workers' minds without relying on actual accidents to maintain awareness.

## Risk Homeostasis

Some researchers propose that people have a target level of risk they're comfortable accepting and that they adjust their behavior to maintain this risk level. When safety improvements reduce obvious risks, people may compensate by taking additional risks in other areas - a phenomenon called risk homeostasis or risk compensation.

While the evidence for risk homeostasis in construction is mixed, the concept highlights the importance of understanding how workers respond to safety interventions. Simply providing better protective equipment may not improve safety if workers respond by working more carelessly.

# Decision Making Under Pressure

Construction work often involves time pressure, physical demands, and complex coordination that can impair decision-making abilities. Understanding how these factors affect human performance helps safety professionals develop more effective approaches to hazard control.

## The Production-Safety Trade-off

Construction workers frequently face situations where the safest approach conflicts with productivity demands. Installing fall protection takes time, following lockout procedures can slow electrical work, and waiting for proper equipment may delay project schedules. These production-safety trade-offs create psychological pressure that can lead to poor safety decisions.

Research shows that when people feel pressured to choose between competing priorities, they often focus on the most immediate and visible consequences while discounting longer-term or less visible risks. A worker facing pressure to complete a task quickly may focus on the immediate consequences of delays while underestimating the long-term consequences of unsafe behavior.

Effective safety programs must acknowledge these trade-offs rather than pretending they don't exist. Solutions might include adjusting project schedules to allow time for safe work practices, providing incentives that reward both safety and productivity, or developing work methods that eliminate conflicts between safety and efficiency.

## Cognitive Load and Attention

Construction work often requires workers to manage multiple complex tasks simultaneously while monitoring changing environmental conditions. This cognitive load can overwhelm workers' attention capacity and lead to safety errors, even among experienced and well-trained workers.

Understanding cognitive load helps explain why safety performance may deteriorate during complex or demanding work activities. It also suggests interventions such as simplifying work procedures, reducing unnecessary distractions, and designing work environments that support rather than compete with safety-related attention demands.

### Stress and Decision Making

Construction work can be physically and psychologically stressful, with workers facing deadline pressure, physical demands, weather challenges, and interpersonal conflicts. Stress affects decision-making by narrowing attention, reducing working memory capacity, and increasing reliance on habitual responses rather than careful analysis.

Chronic stress can also lead to fatigue, which impairs judgment and increases accident risk. Safety professionals must understand how work-related stress affects safety performance and develop strategies to help workers manage stress while maintaining safety focus.

## Social Psychology and Safety Culture

Construction work is inherently social, involving coordination between multiple trades, supervision relationships, and informal peer interactions that significantly influence individual behavior. Understanding these social psychological factors is essential for developing effective safety interventions.

### Social Norms and Peer Influence

People are powerfully influenced by their perceptions of what others do (descriptive norms) and what others approve of (injunctive norms). If workers perceive that their peers regularly take shortcuts or that supervisors don't really care about safety despite official policies, they're likely to adjust their behavior accordingly.

Social norms can either support or undermine formal safety programs. Strong positive safety norms create environments where workers encourage each other to work safely and speak up about hazards. Weak or negative safety norms create environments where workers feel pressured to take risks to fit in or avoid being seen as overly cautious.

Changing social norms requires consistent, visible commitment from leaders and sustained effort to reinforce desired behaviors while discouraging unsafe practices. This process takes time because social norms develop through repeated interactions and shared experiences.

**Authority and Compliance**
Construction work involves clear authority relationships, with supervisors directing worker activities and making decisions about work methods, schedules, and resource allocation. Workers' relationships with authority figures significantly influence their safety behavior.

Research on authority and compliance shows that people are more likely to follow directions from legitimate authority figures, but they're also more likely to comply with unreasonable requests if they perceive strong authority pressure. This dynamic can either support or undermine safety efforts depending on how authority is exercised.

Effective safety leadership involves using authority to support rather than undermine safety objectives. This means consistently prioritizing safety in decision-making, providing workers with the resources and time needed to work safely, and creating environments where workers feel comfortable raising safety concerns without fear of retaliation.

**Group Dynamics and Safety**
Construction crews often develop strong group identities that influence individual behavior. These group dynamics can support safety when crews develop norms of mutual protection and collective responsibility for safety outcomes. However, group dynamics can also undermine safety when crews develop cultures of risk-taking or when individuals feel pressure to prove themselves by taking unnecessary risks.

Understanding group dynamics helps safety professionals develop interventions that leverage positive peer influence while addressing negative group pressures. Effective approaches might include team-based safety training, group goal-setting for safety performance, and recognition programs that celebrate collective safety achievements.

## Motivation and Behavior Change

Creating lasting improvements in safety behavior requires understanding what motivates people to change established patterns of behavior. Human motivation is complex, involving both external factors like rewards and consequences and internal factors like personal values and sense of efficacy.

**Intrinsic vs. Extrinsic Motivation**
Psychologists distinguish between intrinsic motivation, which comes from internal satisfaction with activities themselves, and extrinsic motivation, which comes from external rewards or consequences. While both types of motivation can influence safety behavior, research suggests that intrinsic motivation tends to be more sustainable over time.

Safety programs that rely primarily on external rewards (such as safety bonuses) or punishments (such as disciplinary actions for safety violations) may achieve short-term compliance but may not create lasting behavior change. More effective programs help workers develop intrinsic motivation for safety by connecting safety practices to personal values, professional identity, and sense of craftsmanship.

## Self-Efficacy and Personal Agency

People are more likely to engage in protective behaviors when they believe they have the ability to perform those behaviors effectively (self-efficacy) and that their actions will actually reduce risks (outcome expectancy). Workers who doubt their ability to use safety equipment correctly or who believe that accidents are largely due to bad luck may be less likely to invest effort in safety practices.

Building self-efficacy requires providing workers with the knowledge, skills, and resources they need to work safely, along with opportunities to practice safety behaviors and receive feedback on their performance. It also requires helping workers understand the connection between their actions and safety outcomes.

## Goal Setting and Feedback

Clear, specific goals combined with regular feedback can motivate behavior change and help people maintain new behaviors over time. However, safety goal-setting is more complex than goal-setting in other areas because the ultimate goal - avoiding accidents - involves events that happen infrequently and unpredictably.

Effective safety goal-setting often focuses on leading indicators of safety performance (such as hazard identification, training completion, or near-miss reporting) rather than lagging indicators (such as injury rates). This approach provides more frequent opportunities for feedback and reinforcement while focusing attention on proactive safety behaviors.

## Communication Psychology

Safety professionals spend much of their time communicating - conducting training sessions, investigating accidents, discussing hazards with workers, and presenting safety information to management. Understanding the psychology of communication helps you deliver messages more effectively and build stronger relationships with the people you're trying to influence.

### Message Framing and Persuasion

How you frame safety messages significantly affects how they're received and acted upon. Messages emphasizing potential losses (such as injury consequences) may be effective for some audiences and situations, while messages emphasizing potential gains (such as benefits of safe practices) may be more effective for others.

Research on message framing suggests that loss-framed messages tend to be more effective for promoting prevention behaviors (such as using protective equipment), while gain-framed messages tend to be more effective for promoting detection behaviors (such as participating in health screenings). Understanding these principles helps you craft more persuasive safety communications.

### Trust and Credibility

People are more likely to accept and act on safety messages from sources they perceive as trustworthy and credible. Trust develops through consistency between words and actions, demonstrated competence, and genuine concern for workers' welfare.

Building trust and credibility requires more than

technical expertise. It also requires understanding workers' perspectives, acknowledging the challenges they face, and demonstrating that safety recommendations are practical and achievable given real work constraints.

### Cultural and Individual Differences
Construction workforces are increasingly diverse, with workers from different cultural backgrounds, educational levels, and life experiences. Effective safety communication must account for these differences in values, communication styles, learning preferences, and risk perceptions.

Cultural competence in safety communication involves understanding how different groups perceive authority, respond to direct vs. indirect communication, prefer individual vs. group learning experiences, and balance competing priorities such as individual safety and family economic security.

## Behavioral Safety Approaches
Understanding safety psychology has led to the development of behavioral safety approaches that focus specifically on changing observable safety behaviors through systematic observation, feedback, and reinforcement.

### The ABC Model
Behavioral safety programs often use the ABC model, which analyzes the Antecedents (conditions that precede behavior), Behaviors (observable actions), and Consequences (what happens after behaviors) that influence safety performance.

Antecedents include factors such as training, policies, equipment availability, and work instructions that set the stage for behavior. Behaviors include the specific actions workers take (or fail to take) to protect themselves and others. Consequences include both immediate outcomes (such as supervisor feedback) and longer-term outcomes (such as injuries or recognition).

Effective behavioral safety interventions systematically address all three elements: ensuring that antecedents support safe behavior, clearly defining the specific behaviors that are desired, and providing appropriate consequences that reinforce safe behavior while discouraging unsafe behavior.

## Observation and Feedback
Behavioral safety programs typically involve systematic observation of work activities to identify safe and unsafe behaviors, followed by feedback conversations that reinforce safe behaviors and address unsafe behaviors. These observations are usually conducted by trained observers who use standardized checklists to ensure consistency.

The effectiveness of observation and feedback depends on several factors: the quality of the relationship between observers and workers, the focus on specific behaviors rather than general safety attitudes, the timing and specificity of feedback, and the consistency of the observation process over time.

## Positive Reinforcement
Behavioral safety emphasizes positive reinforcement of safe behaviors rather than punishment of unsafe behaviors. This approach is based on research showing that positive reinforcement tends to be more effective than punishment for creating lasting behavior change.

However, implementing positive reinforcement effectively requires understanding what individuals find reinforcing, ensuring that reinforcement is contingent on desired behaviors, and providing reinforcement frequently enough to maintain behavior change.

## Addressing Resistance to Safety

Despite best efforts, safety professionals often encounter resistance to safety initiatives from workers, supervisors, or management. Understanding the psychological sources of this resistance helps you develop more effective strategies for overcoming it.

### Sources of Resistance

Resistance to safety initiatives can stem from various psychological factors: fear of change, past negative experiences with safety programs, concerns about productivity impacts, skepticism about management motives, or simple habit and routine.

Understanding the specific sources of resistance in your situation helps you develop targeted approaches to address concerns and build support for safety improvements. Generic approaches to overcoming resistance are less effective than approaches tailored to specific concerns and circumstances.

### Building Buy-in and Ownership

People are more likely to support initiatives they helped develop and feel ownership of. Involving workers and supervisors in safety program development, hazard identification, and solution development can reduce resistance while improving the quality of safety initiatives.

Building buy-in requires genuine participation, not just token consultation. People can distinguish between meaningful involvement and superficial participation, and attempts to manipulate participation often backfire by increasing cynicism and resistance.

## Dealing with Chronic Safety Violators

Every workplace has individuals who consistently resist safety requirements despite training, feedback, and disciplinary actions. Understanding the psychology behind chronic safety violations helps you develop more effective approaches to these challenging situations.

Chronic safety violators may be responding to psychological factors such as sensation-seeking personality traits, underlying mental health issues, substance abuse problems, or deep-seated beliefs about personal invulnerability. Addressing these situations often requires individualized approaches that go beyond standard disciplinary procedures.

# Integrating Psychology into Safety Practice

Understanding safety psychology is valuable only if you can translate this knowledge into more effective safety practices. This integration requires developing skills in assessment, intervention design, and evaluation that draw on psychological principles while remaining practical for construction environments.

## Psychological Assessment of Safety Culture

Assessing the psychological factors that influence safety in your organization requires systematic data collection through surveys, interviews, focus groups, and behavioral observations. This assessment should examine factors such as risk perceptions, safety attitudes, social norms, leadership effectiveness, and communication patterns.

Effective assessment goes beyond measuring overall safety

climate to understand the specific psychological factors that support or undermine safety in your particular context. This detailed understanding enables you to design interventions that address root causes rather than just symptoms.

### Designing Psychology-Based Interventions

Effective safety interventions should be based on solid understanding of the psychological factors they're intended to address. This means moving beyond generic safety approaches to develop interventions tailored to specific psychological barriers and motivators in your workplace.

Intervention design should consider factors such as individual differences in learning styles and motivation, group dynamics and social influences, organizational culture and leadership styles, and the broader context in which safety decisions are made.

### Measuring Psychological Outcomes

Evaluating the effectiveness of psychology-based safety interventions requires measuring changes in psychological factors such as attitudes, perceptions, knowledge, and behavioral intentions, not just traditional safety metrics such as injury rates.

These psychological measures can provide early indicators of intervention effectiveness and help you refine approaches before problems become apparent in injury statistics. They also help you understand the mechanisms through which interventions create change, enabling you to replicate successful approaches in other contexts.

## Your Role as a Safety Psychologist

As a construction safety professional, you won't be a trained psychologist, but you will need to apply psychological principles in your daily work. This requires developing skills in observation, communication, and influence that draw on psychological knowledge while remaining authentic to your professional role.

## Developing Psychological Insight

Developing insight into the psychological factors that influence safety requires cultivating observational skills, learning to see situations from others' perspectives, and understanding the complex factors that influence human behavior in work settings.

This insight develops through experience, reflection, and ongoing learning about human behavior. It requires moving beyond superficial explanations for safety problems to understand the underlying psychological factors that create and maintain unsafe behaviors.

## Building Psychological Skills

Effective application of safety psychology requires developing practical skills in areas such as motivational interviewing, conflict resolution, group facilitation, and behavior change counseling. These skills complement your technical safety knowledge and make you more effective at creating lasting safety improvements.

These skills can be developed through formal training, mentoring relationships, and deliberate practice in real workplace situations. They require ongoing refinement based on feedback and reflection on what works in different contexts.

## Ethical Considerations

Applying psychological principles in safety work raises ethical considerations about respect for individual autonomy, informed consent, and the appropriate use of influence techniques. Understanding these ethical issues helps you apply psychological knowledge responsibly and maintain trust with the people you work with.

Ethical practice requires being transparent about your methods, respecting individual differences and choices, and ensuring that psychological approaches serve legitimate safety objectives rather than inappropriate manipulation or control.

## The Future of Safety Psychology

The field of safety psychology continues to evolve as researchers develop better understanding of human factors in safety and practitioners develop more effective applications of psychological principles. Staying current with these developments will help you remain effective throughout your career.

### Emerging Research Areas

Current research in safety psychology is exploring areas such as the neuroscience of risk perception, the role of emotions in safety decision-making, the effects of technology on human performance, and the application of positive psychology principles to safety improvement.

Understanding these emerging areas helps you anticipate future developments in safety practice and identify opportunities to enhance your effectiveness through application of new knowledge.

**Technology and Psychology**
New technologies are creating both opportunities and challenges for applying psychological principles in safety work. Virtual reality training can provide realistic practice opportunities, wearable devices can provide real-time feedback on safety behaviors, and mobile applications can deliver personalized safety communications.

However, technology also creates new challenges such as distraction, over-reliance on automated systems, and reduced face-to-face interaction. Understanding both the opportunities and challenges helps you use technology effectively while maintaining focus on fundamental psychological principles.

# Conclusion: The Human Side of Safety

Construction safety is ultimately about human behavior - the decisions people make, the risks they choose to accept or avoid, and the social dynamics that influence these choices. Technical knowledge about hazards and regulations is essential, but it's not sufficient for creating safe workplaces. You must also understand the psychological factors that influence how people perceive risks, make decisions, and respond to safety interventions.

This understanding doesn't require you to become a psychologist, but it does require you to see safety work as fundamentally concerned with human behavior rather than just technical compliance. The most effective safety professionals are those who combine technical expertise with genuine insight into what motivates people and how to create conditions that support safe behavior.

The psychological principles discussed in this chapter provide a foundation for more effective safety practice, but they must be adapted to your specific context and applied with sensitivity to individual and cultural differences. The goal is not to manipulate or control people, but to create conditions where safe behavior is easier, more rewarding, and more consistent with people's values and goals.

As you develop your career in construction safety, continue to observe and learn about human behavior in work settings. The insights you gain will make you more effective at preventing injuries, building safety culture, and helping construction workers return home safely every day. Remember that behind every safety statistic is a human being making decisions under challenging circumstances - your job is to help them make the safest decisions possible.

# CHAPTER 4: HAZARD RECOGNITION AND RISK ASSESSMENT

*"The best safety professionals don't just react to accidents; they prevent them by seeing what others miss."*

Imagine walking onto a construction site and immediately spotting the loose scaffolding that could collapse, the improperly stored chemicals that could ignite, and the worker operating equipment without proper fall protection. This ability to systematically identify and evaluate hazards before they cause harm is the cornerstone skill that separates exceptional safety professionals from the rest.

Hazard recognition and risk assessment form the foundation of all effective safety programs. Without these skills, you're essentially playing safety defense instead of offense; waiting for incidents to happen rather than preventing them. This chapter will transform how you see construction sites, teaching you to identify hazards with the systematic precision of a detective and assess risks with the analytical rigor of a scientist.

## Understanding Hazards vs. Risks

Before diving into recognition techniques, it's crucial to understand the distinction between hazards and risks; terms often used interchangeably but with important differences.

**A hazard** is any source of potential damage, harm, or adverse health effects. It's the condition or situation that has the potential to cause injury. Think of it as the loaded gun.

**Risk** is the likelihood that a hazard will actually cause harm, combined with the severity of that harm. It's the probability that someone will pull the trigger and the consequences if they do.

### Examples in Construction Context
- **Hazard**: An unguarded excavation 8 feet deep
- **Risk**: High probability of fatal injury if a worker falls in (considering factors like proximity to work areas, visibility, and current safety measures)
- **Hazard**: Electrical wiring exposed during demolition
- **Risk**: Moderate probability of serious injury depending on voltage, weather conditions, and worker training

This distinction matters because it shapes your response. You might encounter hundreds of hazards on a large construction site, but you need to prioritize your efforts based on risk levels.

## The Hierarchy of Controls: Your Strategic Framework

The hierarchy of controls isn't just a safety concept - it's your strategic framework for thinking about hazard mitigation. Understanding this hierarchy will shape how you approach every risk assessment and guide your recommendations.

## 1. Elimination
**Concept**: Completely remove the hazard from the workplace.
**Construction Examples**:
- Using prefabricated components assembled at ground level instead of working at height
- Substituting a less hazardous demolition method
- Redesigning a process to eliminate a dangerous step

**When to Use**: Always consider this first. While often seen as impractical, creative thinking can reveal elimination opportunities others miss.

## 2. Substitution
**Concept**: Replace the hazard with something less dangerous.
**Construction Examples**:
- Using water-based instead of solvent-based coatings
- Choosing pneumatic tools over electric tools in wet conditions
- Selecting lighter materials that reduce manual handling risks

**Key Insight**: Substitution requires understanding the underlying function, not just the obvious solution.

## 3. Engineering Controls
**Concept**: Isolate people from the hazard through design or equipment. **Construction Examples**:
- Guardrails around elevated work areas
- Ventilation systems for confined spaces
- Machine guards on equipment
- Sound barriers around noisy operations

**Why They're Effective**: They don't rely on human behavior to be effective - they work automatically.

## 4. Administrative Controls
**Concept**: Change how people work through policies, training, and procedures. **Construction Examples**:
- Job rotation to limit exposure time
- Lockout/tagout procedures
- Confined space entry permits
- Safety training programs

**Critical Limitation**: These controls depend entirely on human compliance and can fail if not consistently enforced.

## 5. Personal Protective Equipment (PPE)
**Concept**: Equipment worn by individuals to reduce exposure to hazards. **Construction Examples**:
- Hard hats, safety glasses, hearing protection
- Fall protection harnesses
- Respiratory protection
- Cut-resistant gloves

**Important Reality**: PPE is your last line of defense, not your first choice. It protects only the person wearing it and fails if not used correctly.

## Applying the Hierarchy Strategically
The hierarchy isn't just a checklist - it's a thinking tool. When you encounter a hazard, mentally work through each level:
1. "Can we eliminate this entirely?"
2. "If not, can we substitute something safer?"
3. "Can we engineer a solution that doesn't rely on human behavior?"
4. "What administrative controls do we need?"
5. "What PPE is required as backup protection?"

Often, the most effective solutions combine multiple levels. For example, working at height might involve:
- **Elimination**: Using mobile elevated work platforms instead of ladders
- **Engineering**: Guardrails on the platform
- **Administrative**: Operator training and inspection procedures
- **PPE**: Fall protection harnesses as backup

# Conducting Effective Job Hazard Analyses (JHAs)

The Job Hazard Analysis is your systematic approach to breaking down work activities and identifying associated hazards. Think of it as creating a safety roadmap for any task.

## The JHA Process: A Step-by-Step Approach

### Step 1: Select the Job

**Priority Jobs for Analysis**:
- Jobs with the highest injury rates
- Jobs with potential for severe injuries or fatalities
- New jobs or jobs with changed procedures
- Jobs performed infrequently where workers may be rusty

**Pro Tip**: Start with jobs where you can make the biggest impact. Success with high-visibility or high-risk jobs builds credibility for your safety program.

### Step 2: Break the Job into Steps

Break the job down into sequential steps, but avoid being too detailed or too general. Aim for 8-12 steps for most jobs.

**Example: Installing Roof Trusses**
1. Position crane and establish work area
2. Attach lifting rigging to truss
3. Signal crane operator to lift truss

4. Guide truss into position
5. Secure truss to building structure
6. Remove lifting rigging
7. Install temporary bracing
8. Move to next truss location

**Common Mistake**: Listing steps like "be careful" or "work safely." Focus on specific actions, not safety advice.

### Step 3: Identify Hazards for Each Step
For each step, ask yourself:
- What could go wrong?
- What are the consequences?
- How could it happen?

**Hazard Categories to Consider**:
- **Struck by/against**: Moving objects, equipment, materials
- **Fall hazards**: Heights, same level, into excavations
- **Caught in/between**: Machinery, collapsing materials
- **Electrical**: Contact with power lines, faulty equipment
- **Chemical**: Toxic substances, skin/eye contact
- **Ergonomic**: Lifting, repetitive motions, awkward positions
- **Environmental**: Weather, noise, temperature extremes

### Step 4: Develop Controls
For each identified hazard, determine controls using the hierarchy. Be specific about what will be done, who will do it, and when.

**Example Control Development**:
- **Hazard**: Worker could fall while positioning truss (Step 4)
- **Controls**:

- Engineering: Install safety nets below work area
- Administrative: Only certified riggers guide trusses
- PPE: Full body harness with shock-absorbing lanyard

**Making JHAs Living Documents**
The best JHAs aren't filed away and forgotten - they become working tools that evolve with experience.
**Implementation Strategies:**
- Involve workers who actually perform the job in the analysis
- Review and update JHAs when incidents occur or procedures change
- Use JHAs during toolbox talks and job briefings
- Post relevant JHA sections at job locations
- Train supervisors to reference JHAs during job planning

**Digital Integration**: Modern construction companies are moving JHAs to mobile platforms, allowing real-time updates and photo documentation of hazard conditions.

# Risk Matrix Development and Application

A risk matrix is your tool for quantifying and prioritizing risks consistently across different jobs and hazards. It transforms subjective risk perception into objective decision-making criteria.

## Building Your Risk Matrix
### Severity Scale (Consequences)

**Level 1 - Minor**: First aid injury, minimal property damage, brief work interruption
- *Example*: Small cut requiring bandage

**Level 2 - Moderate**: Medical treatment injury, moderate property damage, work interruption up to 1 day
- *Example*: Sprained ankle requiring medical evaluation

**Level 3 - Major**: Lost time injury, significant property damage, work interruption 1-7 days
- *Example*: Broken bone requiring hospitalization

**Level 4 - Severe**: Permanent disability, major property damage, work shutdown over 1 week
- *Example*: Amputation or permanent back injury

**Level 5 - Catastrophic**: Fatality, facility destruction, indefinite shutdown
- *Example*: Fatal fall or electrocution

### Probability Scale (Likelihood)

**Level 1 - Rare**: May occur in exceptional circumstances (less than once in 10 years)

**Level 2 - Unlikely**: Could occur but not expected (once in 5-10 years)

**Level 3 - Possible**: Might occur occasionally (once in 1-5 years)

**Level 4 - Likely**: Expected to occur regularly (once per year)

**Level 5 - Almost Certain**: Expected to occur frequently (multiple times per year)

## Risk Rating Calculation
### Risk Score = Severity × Probability

| Risk Score | Risk Level | Action Required |
|---|---|---|
| 1-5 | Low | Monitor, standard precautions |
| 6-12 | Medium | Additional controls needed |

| 13-20 | High | Immediate action required |
| 21-25 | Extreme | Stop work until controls implemented |

## Practical Application Example

**Scenario**: Workers installing electrical conduit on scaffolding 15 feet high

**Hazard Analysis**:
 Hazard: Fall from scaffolding
 Severity: 4 (Falls from this height can result in death)
 Probability: 4 (Falls are frequent in construction, especially when guardrails/PPE are absent)
 Risk Score: 4 x 4 = 16 (High Risk)

**Required Actions**:
- Immediate implementation of fall protection
- Enhanced scaffolding inspection procedures
- Additional worker training
- Consider alternative methods (aerial lifts, prefabrication)

## Common Pitfalls in Risk Assessment

**Optimism Bias**: Consistently rating probability lower than reality because "it won't happen to us." Combat this by using historical data and incident reports from similar operations.

**Familiarity Breeds Complacency**: Rating familiar hazards as lower risk simply because workers are used to them. Some of the most dangerous situations are routine activities done without proper precautions.

**Single Point Assessment**: Evaluating risks in isolation rather than considering cumulative effects. Multiple moderate risks can combine to create high-risk situations.

# Documentation and Follow-up Procedures

Effective documentation transforms your hazard recognition and risk assessment from one-time exercises into systematic safety management tools.

## Essential Documentation Elements
### The Hazard Register
Maintain a comprehensive database of all identified hazards, including:
- **Location and description** of hazard
- **Date identified** and by whom
- **Risk assessment** (initial and current)
- **Controls implemented** (with dates)
- **Responsible parties** for ongoing monitoring
- **Review dates** and assessment updates

### Risk Assessment Reports
Each formal risk assessment should include:
- **Scope and methodology** used
- **Personnel involved** in the assessment
- **Assumptions and limitations**
- **Detailed findings** with supporting evidence
- **Recommended controls** with implementation timelines
- **Residual risk levels** after controls
- **Review and update schedule**

## Follow-up Systems That Work
### The Control Verification Process
**30-Day Check**: Verify that recommended controls have been implemented as planned.

**90-Day Assessment**: Evaluate the effectiveness of implemented controls.

**Annual Review**: Comprehensive reassessment of all high and medium risks.

## Tracking Metrics
- **Hazard identification rate**: Number of hazards identified per site inspection
- **Control implementation rate**: Percentage of recommended controls actually implemented
- **Risk reduction achievement**: Average reduction in risk scores after control implementation
- **Overdue action items**: Number and age of unresolved high-risk items

## Technology Integration
Modern construction sites increasingly use digital tools to enhance documentation and follow-up:
**Mobile Apps**: Allow real-time hazard reporting with photos and GPS coordinates **Cloud-based Systems**: Enable instant sharing of risk assessments across project teams **Automated Alerts**: Notify responsible parties when action items are overdue **Dashboard Reporting**: Provide visual summaries of risk status across multiple projects.

---

# Practical Exercises
### Exercise 1: Hazard Recognition Walk
**Objective**: Develop systematic hazard recognition skills
**Setup**: Use the provided construction site photograph or visit an actual construction site.

**Process**:
1. Spend 2 minutes scanning the scene and noting obvious hazards
2. Spend 5 minutes using systematic observation:
    - Ground level hazards
    - Elevated work hazards
    - Equipment and machinery hazards
    - Environmental hazards

- Human behavior hazards
3. Compare your initial 2-minute list with your systematic 5-minute assessment

**Debrief Questions**:
- How many additional hazards did systematic observation reveal?
- Which hazard categories were you most likely to miss initially?
- What does this tell you about the importance of structured observation?

## Exercise 2: JHA Development

**Scenario**: Develop a complete JHA for "Installing Windows in a Second-Story Opening"

**Your Task**:
1. Break the job into 7-10 sequential steps
2. Identify at least 2 hazards for each step
3. Develop specific controls using the hierarchy of controls
4. Assign risk ratings to each identified hazard

**Success Criteria**:
- Each step describes a specific action, not a safety precaution
- Hazards are specific and realistic for construction work
- Controls address the actual hazards identified
- Risk ratings are consistent and defensible

## Exercise 3: Risk Matrix Application

**Scenario**: You've identified the following hazards on a bridge construction project:

1. Worker exposure to traffic while setting up work zone
2. Potential for tools to be dropped from bridge deck
3. River current creating hazard for boat traffic below
4. Crane operation near overhead power lines
5. Concrete truck backing up in congested area

**Your Task**:
1. Assign severity and probability ratings to each hazard
2. Calculate risk scores and determine required action levels
3. Prioritize the hazards for control implementation
4. Justify your ratings with specific reasoning

# Case Study: The Near-Miss That Changed Everything
## Background
Martinez Construction was renovating a 12-story office building in downtown Phoenix. The project involved significant structural modifications, including removing interior walls and installing new steel beams. The company had a decent safety record - no fatalities in five years and OSHA injury rates slightly below industry average.
## The Incident
On a Tuesday morning in March, structural engineer Sarah Chen was conducting her weekly inspection when she noticed something that made her stop cold. A crew was preparing to remove a load-bearing wall on the 8th floor, but the temporary support system looked inadequate. The shoring appeared to be rated for much less load than what the structural drawings indicated would be required.

Chen immediately halted the work and called for the project manager. Upon investigation, they discovered a cascade of

failures:
1. The original structural analysis had been based on outdated building drawings
2. The JHA for wall removal hadn't included a structural engineer's review
3. The shoring equipment had been selected by availability, not engineering requirements
4. The crew supervisor had noticed the shoring "looked light" but hadn't raised concerns

## The Analysis
**What the risk assessment revealed**:
- **Hazard**: Structural collapse during wall removal
- **Severity**: 5 (Catastrophic - potential for multiple fatalities)
- **Initial Probability**: 4 (Likely - inadequate shoring would almost certainly fail)
- **Risk Score**: 20 (Extreme Risk)

**Root causes identified**:
- Inadequate hazard analysis process for complex structural work
- Missing technical review requirements in JHA procedures
- Weak stop-work authority culture among field supervisors
- Insufficient communication between engineering and field teams

## The Transformation
This near-miss led Martinez Construction to completely overhaul their hazard recognition and risk assessment processes:

**Process Changes**:
1. **Mandatory Technical Reviews**: All JHAs for

structural work now require engineering sign-off
2. **Enhanced Stop-Work Authority**: Field supervisors receive specific training on recognizing when to halt work
3. **Collaborative Risk Assessment**: Weekly sessions involving engineers, supervisors, and craft workers
4. **Digital Integration**: Mobile apps allow real-time consultation with technical experts

**Cultural Changes**:
1. **Near-Miss Celebration**: Workers who identify potential catastrophic hazards receive recognition, not blame
2. **Engineering Accessibility**: Structural engineers spend minimum 2 hours daily on active construction floors
3. **Questioning Attitude**: "Does this look right?" becomes an encouraged question, not a sign of inexperience

## Results
Eighteen months after implementing these changes:
- Hazard identification rate increased by 300%
- High-risk situations caught and corrected before work started increased by 250%
- Worker safety survey scores improved significantly
- Zero structural-related incidents or near-misses
- Client satisfaction increased due to proactive problem-solving approach

## Lessons for Safety Professionals
1. **Technical Competence Matters**: Understanding the work being performed is crucial for effective hazard

recognition
2. **Process Failures Cascade**: One weak link in hazard analysis can create extreme risks
3. **Culture Trumps Procedures**: The best risk assessment process fails without a culture that supports it
4. **Near-Misses Are Gold**: They provide learning opportunities without the cost of actual harm

## Chapter Summary

Hazard recognition and risk assessment form the foundation of effective construction safety management. This chapter has equipped you with:

**Core Concepts**:
- The critical distinction between hazards and risks
- The hierarchy of controls as your strategic framework
- Risk matrices as tools for consistent decision-making

**Practical Skills**:
- Systematic approaches to Job Hazard Analysis
- Documentation systems that support ongoing safety management
- Follow-up procedures that ensure control effectiveness

**Professional Development**:
- Exercise sets that build recognition skills through practice
- Case study analysis that reveals how theory applies in real situations
- Understanding of how hazard recognition fits into broader safety culture

Remember: Hazard recognition is not a one-time skill you master, but a capability you continuously develop. The best safety professionals remain students throughout their careers, constantly refining their ability to see what others miss and assess what others overlook.

As you progress in your safety career, you'll find that hazard recognition becomes almost intuitive - but never casual. The systematic approaches outlined in this chapter will become second nature, allowing you to focus your mental energy on the complex judgment calls that separate good safety professionals from exceptional ones.

In our next chapter, we'll build on this foundation by exploring Personal Protective Equipment - your understanding of hazard recognition will directly inform how you select, implement, and manage PPE programs that truly protect workers rather than just check compliance boxes.

## Key Takeaways

- **Hazards are conditions; risks are probabilities** - This distinction shapes how you prioritize and respond
- **The hierarchy of controls guides strategy** - Always consider elimination and substitution before jumping to PPE
- **JHAs are roadmaps, not checklists** - They should guide thinking, not replace it
- **Risk matrices enable consistent decisions** - But they require honest, data-driven assessments
- **Documentation creates continuity** - Your hazard recognition becomes organizational knowledge
- **Practice develops intuition** - Systematic observation skills improve with deliberate practice
- **Culture enables process** - The best technical tools fail without supportive organizational culture

# CHAPTER 5: PERSONAL PROTECTIVE EQUIPMENT (PPE)

*"PPE doesn't make dangerous work safe; it makes safe work safer."*

Walk onto any construction site and you'll see hard hats, safety vests, and work boots - the universal symbols of construction safety. But here's what separates novice safety professionals from experienced ones: understanding that PPE is simultaneously the most visible and most misunderstood aspect of construction safety.

PPE represents your last line of defense, not your first choice for protection. Yet when properly selected, implemented, and managed, it becomes an essential component of comprehensive safety programs. The challenge isn't just getting workers to wear PPE - it's ensuring they have the right equipment, understand why they need it, and can use it effectively to protect themselves and return home safely each day.

This chapter will transform your understanding of PPE from simple compliance checking to strategic safety management. You'll learn to select equipment based on actual hazard analysis, implement programs that workers embrace rather than endure, and manage PPE as a dynamic system that evolves with your workplace hazards.

## The Strategic Role of PPE in Safety Programs

Before diving into specific equipment types, it's crucial to understand where PPE fits in your overall safety strategy. Remember the hierarchy of controls from Chapter 4? PPE sits at the bottom for good reason - but that doesn't make it unimportant.

**Why PPE is Last Resort (But Still Essential)**
**Limitations of PPE:**
- Protects only the individual wearing it
- Effectiveness depends entirely on proper use
- Can fail without warning
- Requires ongoing maintenance and replacement
- May create new hazards (heat stress, reduced visibility, communication barriers)

**When PPE Becomes Primary Protection:**
- Hazards cannot be eliminated or engineered out
- During emergency response situations
- Short-duration, high-risk activities
- Mobile work where engineering controls aren't feasible
- As backup protection for critical hazards

**The PPE Program Philosophy**
Effective PPE programs are built on three fundamental

principles:

1. **Hazard-Driven Selection**: Equipment is chosen based on specific hazard analysis, not generic requirements or what's cheapest.

2. **User-Centered Design**: Programs consider the human factors that determine whether PPE will actually be used correctly.

3. **Systematic Management**: PPE is managed as an integrated system with clear procedures for selection, training, maintenance, and replacement.

## Selection Criteria for Different Hazards

The most common PPE failures don't happen because equipment breaks - they happen because the wrong equipment was selected for the hazard. Proper selection requires understanding both the specific hazards present and the performance capabilities of available equipment.

### Head Protection: Beyond the Basic Hard Hat
**Hazard Categories**:
- **Impact**: Falling or flying objects
- **Penetration**: Sharp objects falling from above
- **Electrical**: Contact with energized conductors
- **Bump**: Low-hanging obstacles in confined spaces

**Selection Criteria**:
**Type I vs. Type II Hard Hats**:
- **Type I**: Top impact and penetration resistance only
- **Type II**: Top and lateral impact protection (essential for electrical work)

**Class Designations**:
- **Class E (Electrical)**: Tested to 20,000 volts, dielectric protection
- **Class G (General)**: Tested to 2,200 volts, limited

electrical protection
- **Class C (Conductive)**: No electrical protection, often lightweight for comfort

**Application Examples**:
- **Concrete work**: Type I, Class G with chin strap for windy conditions
- **Electrical installation**: Type II, Class E with face shield attachment points
- **Steel erection**: Type I, Class G with sweatband for extended wear
- **Confined space**: Lightweight bump caps or Type I with lamp brackets

**Advanced Considerations**:
- **Ventilation**: Vented hard hats for hot environments vs. non-vented for rain protection
- **Accessory compatibility**: Ensure hard hat can accommodate required face shields, hearing protection, headlamps
- **Replacement indicators**: Some modern hard hats include UV exposure indicators showing when replacement is needed

## Eye and Face Protection: Seeing the Differences
### Hazard Analysis Framework:
- **Impact**: Flying particles, fragments
- **Chemical splash**: Liquids, vapors, gases
- **Radiation**: Welding, cutting, UV exposure
- **Heat**: Molten metal, hot gases
- **Dust**: Fine particles, debris

**Safety Glasses vs. Goggles vs. Face Shields**:
**Safety Glasses**:
- **Best for**: General impact protection, extended wear comfort

- **Limitations**: Side protection varies, no splash protection
- **Selection factors**: Lens material (polycarbonate vs. Trivex), anti-fog coatings, prescription compatibility

**Safety Goggles**:
- **Best for**: Chemical splash, dust protection, over-prescription glasses
- **Types**: Direct vent (impact only), indirect vent (chemical splash), non-vented (chemical/gas protection)
- **Fit considerations**: Foam padding, elastic vs. fabric straps, lens replacement capability

**Face Shields**:
- **Best for**: Full face protection from splash, impact, heat
- **Critical requirement**: Must be worn WITH safety glasses or goggles
- **Selection factors**: Lens material thickness, optical clarity, attachment method

**Specialized Applications**:
**Welding Protection**:
- **Shade selection**: Based on amperage and process (MIG, TIG, stick, oxy-fuel)
- **Auto-darkening vs. passive**: Battery life, switching speed, sensitivity adjustment
- **Coverage area**: Full helmet vs. hand-held shields vs. clip-on attachments

**Laser Protection**:
- **Wavelength-specific**: Must match laser type exactly
- **Optical density**: Based on laser power and exposure duration
- **Certification**: Ensure ANSI Z136.1 compliance

## Respiratory Protection: When Air Quality Matters

Respiratory protection represents one of the most complex

areas of PPE selection, requiring understanding of both contaminant characteristics and physiological factors.

**Contaminant Classification**:
- **Particulates**: Dust, fibers, fumes (measured in microns)
- **Gases**: Molecular contaminants (carbon monoxide, hydrogen sulfide)
- **Vapors**: Evaporated liquids (solvents, fuels)
- **Oxygen deficiency**: Less than 19.5% oxygen by volume

**Protection Factor Concept**: Protection Factor = Ambient Concentration ÷ Concentration Inside Respirator

**Assigned Protection Factors (APF)**:
- **Disposable filtering facepiece**: APF 10
- **Half-face elastomeric**: APF 10
- **Full-face elastomeric**: APF 50
- **Powered air-purifying (PAPR)**: APF 25-1000 depending on design
- **Supplied air**: APF 50-10,000 depending on configuration

**Selection Decision Tree**:

**Step 1: Oxygen Level Assessment**
- If $O_2$ < 19.5%: Supplied air required (never use air-purifying respirators)
- If $O_2$ ≥ 19.5%: Proceed to contaminant analysis

**Step 2: Contaminant Identification**
- Identify all airborne hazards present
- Determine concentrations through air sampling
- Check for skin absorption hazards (require full-face protection)

**Step 3: Protection Factor Calculation**

- Calculate required PF: Ambient Concentration ÷ Exposure Limit
- Select respirator with APF ≥ Required PF
- Apply safety factor (typically 10x minimum)

**Step 4: Fit and User Factors**
- Facial hair compatibility (full-face may be required)
- Communication requirements
- Physical demands of work
- Duration of use

**Common Construction Applications:**
**Silica Dust (Concrete cutting, sandblasting):**
- **Minimum**: N95 filtering facepiece for short exposures
- **Preferred**: Half-face with P100 filters
- **High exposure**: PAPR with HEPA filters or supplied air

**Asbestos Removal:**
- **Minimum**: Full-face with HEPA filters (APF 50)
- **Preferred**: PAPR with full facepiece (APF 1000)
- **Note**: Requires complete respiratory protection program

**Welding Fumes:**
- **Light duty**: Disposable with nuisance-level organic vapor relief
- **Heavy duty**: Half-face with P95 filters
- **Confined space**: Supplied air with escape respirator

## Hand Protection: Complexity of Glove Selection

Hand injuries account for approximately 25% of all workplace injuries, making hand protection critical. However, gloves also affect dexterity, grip, and tactile sensitivity, requiring careful balance between protection and functionality.

**Hazard Categories and Materials:**
**Cut and Puncture Resistance:**
- **ANSI/ISEA 105 levels**: A1 (lowest) through A9 (highest)
- **Materials**: HPPE (high-performance polyethylene), Kevlar, metal mesh
- **Applications**: Glass handling (A4-A6), metal fabrication (A6-A8), demolition (A7-A9)

**Chemical Resistance:**
- **Breakthrough time**: How long chemical takes to permeate glove material
- **Permeation rate**: Speed of chemical movement through material after breakthrough
- **Material selection**: Nitrile (oils, petroleum), neoprene (acids, alcohols), butyl (gases, ketones), PVC (acids, bases)

**Heat and Cold Protection:**
- **Contact heat**: Leather for brief contact, aluminized for extreme heat
- **Radiant heat**: Reflective materials, multiple layers
- **Cold protection**: Insulation levels, dexterity ratings at temperature

**Electrical Protection:**
- **Voltage ratings**: Class 00 (500V) through Class 4 (36,000V)
- **AC vs. DC ratings**: Different test standards
- **Inspection requirements**: Visual inspection before each use, electrical testing every 6 months

**Selection Methodology:**
**Step 1: Comprehensive Hazard Assessment**
- Identify all hand hazards in work environment
- Prioritize based on severity and frequency
- Consider secondary hazards (grip loss, reduced dexterity)

**Step 2: Performance Requirements**

- Protection level needed for each hazard
- Dexterity requirements for task performance
- Duration of use and comfort factors
- Contamination and laundering considerations

**Step 3: Multi-Hazard Integration**
- Select gloves that protect against multiple hazards when possible
- Use glove systems (liner + outer glove) for complex exposures
- Establish glove change-out procedures for contamination control

**Common Construction Combinations**:
- **General construction**: Cut-resistant (A2-A3) with grip coating
- **Concrete work**: Chemical-resistant with cut protection and grip
- **Electrical work**: Leather protectors over electrical-rated rubber gloves
- **Welding**: Heat-resistant leather with reinforced palms and extended cuffs

## Foot Protection: Foundation of Worker Safety
**Hazard Categories**:
- **Compression**: Heavy objects falling on feet
- **Puncture**: Nails, sharp objects penetrating sole
- **Electrical**: Contact with energized sources
- **Chemical**: Splash, immersion in hazardous substances
- **Heat**: Molten metal, hot surfaces
- **Slip/fall**: Inadequate traction on surfaces

**ASTM F2413 Classifications**:
**Impact and Compression**:
- **I**: Impact resistance (75 foot-pounds)
- **C**: Compression resistance (2,500 pounds)
- **Most construction work**: Requires both I and C ratings

**Electrical Hazard**:
- **EH**: Electrical hazard protection (18,000 volts, 60 Hz, 1 minute)
- **Note**: Does not replace other electrical safety procedures

**Puncture Resistance**:
- **PR**: Puncture-resistant sole (270 pounds force)
- **Essential for**: Demolition, roofing, areas with debris

**Specialized Features**:

**Metatarsal Guards**:
- **External**: Removable, adjustable
- **Internal**: Integrated into boot design
- **Applications**: Steel erection, heavy equipment operation

**Slip Resistance**:
- **Outsole design**: Tread pattern, material composition
- **Testing standards**: ASTM F1677, F2913 for different surface conditions
- **Applications**: Wet surfaces, oily conditions, outdoor work

**Selection Considerations**:
- **Fit**: Proper sizing prevents blisters, fatigue
- **Break-in period**: Leather boots require gradual conditioning
- **Maintenance**: Cleaning, conditioning, sole inspection
- **Replacement indicators**: Sole wear, upper damage, loss of water resistance

---

# Proper Use, Maintenance, and Storage

Having the right PPE is only half the battle - ensuring it's used correctly and maintained properly determines whether it actually protects workers.

## The Human Factors Challenge
**Why Workers Don't Wear PPE:**
- **Discomfort**: Poor fit, heat buildup, restricted movement
- **Inconvenience**: Difficult to don/doff, interferes with work
- **Perception**: "It won't happen to me" mentality
- **Peer pressure**: Not wearing PPE to fit in with crew
- **Inadequate training**: Don't understand proper use or importance

**Design Solutions:**
- **Comfort features**: Moisture-wicking materials, ventilation, adjustable fit
- **Convenience features**: Quick-release mechanisms, integrated designs
- **Durability**: Equipment that withstands work environment abuse
- **Appearance**: Professional-looking equipment workers are proud to wear

## Proper Use Procedures
**Donning (Putting On) Procedures:**
**General Sequence** (adjust based on specific hazards):
1. **Inspect equipment** for damage, contamination, proper function
2. **Hand protection first** (protects hands during subsequent donning)
3. **Respiratory protection** (establish clean air supply)
4. **Eye/face protection** (after respiratory to prevent fogging)
5. **Head protection** (may require adjustment after other PPE)

6. **Final check** for gaps, interference, comfort

**Specific Techniques:**
**Respirator Donning:**
1. Cup respirator in hand with nosepiece toward fingertips
2. Position under chin with nosepiece up
3. Pull top strap over head, position high on crown
4. Pull bottom strap over head, position at base of neck
5. Mold nosepiece with both hands (fingertips only)
6. Perform positive and negative pressure checks

**Hard Hat Adjustment:**
1. Measure head circumference at forehead level
2. Adjust suspension system for snug, stable fit
3. Ensure 1-1.25 inch space between head and shell
4. Position front of hat 1 inch above eyebrows
5. Secure chin strap if required for work conditions

**Doffing (Removing) Procedures:**
**Contamination Control:**
- Remove most contaminated items first
- Avoid touching contaminated surfaces with bare hands
- Use specific sequences for biological/chemical contamination
- Wash hands thoroughly after PPE removal

**Order for Chemical Contamination** (most to least contaminated):
1. Outer gloves (if worn)
2. Face shield or goggles
3. Respirator (touch only straps/ties)
4. Inner gloves
5. Wash hands/face before removing remaining PPE

## Maintenance and Storage Systems
**Inspection Protocols:**
**Pre-use Inspection** (every time before use):
- **Visual inspection**: Cracks, holes, wear, contamination
- **Functional testing**: Adjustments, seals, moving parts
- **Cleanliness check**: Previous user contamination
- **Documentation**: Inspection tags, logbooks for complex equipment

**Periodic Detailed Inspection:**
- **Respirators**: Monthly for elastomeric, before each use for disposable
- **Fall protection**: Before each use, detailed monthly, annual by competent person
- **Electrical PPE**: Visual before each use, electrical testing per OSHA schedule
- **Hard hats**: Replace every 5 years or per manufacturer recommendations

**Cleaning and Decontamination:**
**General Principles:**
- Use manufacturer-approved cleaning agents only
- Separate cleaning areas to prevent cross-contamination
- Air dry completely before storage
- Replace equipment that cannot be adequately cleaned

**Specific Procedures:**
**Respirator Cleaning:**
1. Disassemble components (remove filters, valves)
2. Wash facepiece in warm water with mild detergent
3. Rinse thoroughly with clean water
4. Air dry completely (heat drying damages elastomers)
5. Reassemble with new filters/cartridges
6. Store in clean, dry container

**Hard Hat Maintenance**:
- Clean with mild soap and warm water
- Avoid petroleum-based cleaners (weaken plastic)
- Replace suspension system annually or when stretched
- UV exposure indicator systems show when replacement needed

**Storage Requirements**:
**Environmental Factors**:
- **Temperature**: Avoid extreme heat/cold that damages materials
- **Humidity**: Prevent mold/mildew in fabric components
- **Light**: UV exposure degrades many PPE materials
- **Contamination**: Clean storage prevents contamination pickup

**Storage System Design**:
- **Individual assignment**: Each worker has designated storage
- **Clean/dirty separation**: Contaminated equipment segregated
- **Accessibility**: Easy access encourages proper storage
- **Inventory control**: Track equipment condition and replacement needs

**Example Storage Setup**:
- **Personal lockers**: Individual PPE assignment with name tags
- **Cleaning station**: Wash basin, approved cleaning supplies, drying rack
- **Inspection area**: Good lighting, inspection checklists, rejection tags
- **Replacement stock**: Common sizes readily available

## Replacement Criteria and Schedules
**Immediate Replacement Situations**:

- **Visible damage**: Cracks, holes, significant wear
- **Contamination**: Cannot be adequately cleaned
- **Functional failure**: Adjustments don't work, seals fail
- **Hygiene concerns**: Odor, visible soiling, previous user contamination

**Scheduled Replacement Programs:**
**Hard Hats:**
- **Standard**: 5 years from manufacture date
- **Heavy use**: 2-3 years or based on UV exposure indicators
- **Impact damage**: Immediate replacement even if no visible crack

**Safety Glasses/Goggles:**
- **Lenses**: Replace when scratched enough to impair vision
- **Frames**: Replace when no longer provide secure fit
- **Anti-fog coatings**: Replace when coating effectiveness degrades

**Respirators:**
- **Elastomeric facepieces**: Replace when elastomer becomes hard/cracked
- **Filters/cartridges**: Replace based on breakthrough, breathing resistance, or schedule
- **Disposable**: Single use or single day maximum

**Gloves:**
- **Cut-resistant**: Replace when protection level degrades (cut testing available)
- **Chemical-resistant**: Replace based on exposure time and breakthrough data
- **General purpose**: Replace when worn through or grip compromised

# Training Workers on PPE Compliance

The most sophisticated PPE program fails if workers don't understand how to use equipment properly or why it's necessary. Effective training goes beyond simple compliance to create genuine understanding and commitment.

## Adult Learning Principles for PPE Training
**Learning Preferences in Construction**:
- **Visual learners**: Demonstrations, diagrams, before/after photos
- **Kinesthetic learners**: Hands-on practice, equipment manipulation
- **Social learners**: Group discussions, peer experiences
- **Problem-solvers**: Real scenarios, "what would you do" situations

**Motivation Factors**:
- **Personal relevance**: "How does this protect YOU?"
- **Family connections**: "Going home safe to your family"
- **Peer respect**: "Professional workers use professional equipment"
- **Job security**: "Injuries hurt your ability to work and earn"

## Comprehensive Training Program Structure
**Phase 1: Foundation Knowledge** (30-45 minutes)
- **Why PPE matters**: Injury statistics, real case studies
- **How PPE works**: Protection mechanisms, limitations
- **Legal requirements**: OSHA standards, employer responsibilities
- **Program overview**: Company policies, procedures, resources

**Phase 2: Equipment-Specific Training** (45-60 minutes per major category)
- **Hazard recognition**: What hazards does this

equipment address?
- **Selection criteria**: How to choose right equipment for the job
- **Proper use**: Step-by-step donning/doffing procedures
- **Maintenance**: Inspection, cleaning, storage requirements
- **Limitations**: What this equipment does NOT protect against

**Phase 3: Hands-On Practice** (60-90 minutes)
- **Equipment familiarization**: Handle and adjust all PPE types
- **Donning/doffing practice**: Multiple repetitions with coaching
- **Fit testing**: Proper fit achievement for each worker
- **Problem-solving**: What to do when equipment doesn't fit/work right
- **Inspection practice**: Identify damaged or defective equipment

**Phase 4: Job-Specific Integration** (30-45 minutes)
- **Hazard mapping**: PPE requirements for specific job tasks
- **Sequence planning**: How to manage multiple PPE types efficiently
- **Environmental factors**: Heat stress, communication, mobility considerations
- **Emergency procedures**: PPE considerations during emergencies

## Making Training Stick
### Reinforcement Strategies:
### Visual Reminders:
- **Toolbox talks**: Weekly 5-minute PPE topics
- **Posters and signs**: High-visibility locations with key messages
- **Equipment labeling**: Care and use instructions on equipment
- **Digital displays**: Rotating safety messages, injury statistics

**Peer Influence:**
- **Safety champions**: Respected workers who model proper PPE use
- **Crew competitions**: Teams compete on PPE compliance rates
- **Recognition programs**: Acknowledge workers who consistently use PPE properly
- **New worker mentoring**: Experienced workers guide newcomers

**Supervisor Reinforcement:**
- **Daily expectations**: Supervisors check PPE during morning briefings
- **Positive reinforcement**: Praise proper use more than criticizing violations
- **Problem-solving support**: Help workers overcome PPE challenges
- **Consistent enforcement**: Fair, consistent application of PPE policies

**Refresher Training Schedule:**
- **Annual comprehensive**: Full program review and update
- **Quarterly focused**: Deep dive on specific equipment types
- **Monthly toolbox talks**: Brief, targeted topics
- **Incident-triggered**: Additional training after PPE-related incidents

## Addressing Common Training Challenges
**"PPE is Uncomfortable":**
- **Acknowledge the reality**: Don't dismiss comfort concerns
- **Explore solutions**: Different brands, sizes, styles available
- **Gradual adaptation**: Build up wearing time for heavy equipment
- **Peer testimonials**: Workers who found comfortable solutions

**"PPE Slows Me Down"**:
- **Time studies**: Actual vs. perceived time impact
- **Efficiency techniques**: Faster donning/doffing methods
- **Tool integration**: Equipment designed to work with PPE
- **Injury time comparison**: Time off work vs. time to use PPE

**"I've Never Been Hurt Before"**:
- **Statistics reality**: Most injuries happen to experienced workers
- **Case studies**: Real incidents involving experienced workers
- **Near-miss discussions**: Times PPE prevented injury
- **Career longevity**: Staying healthy for long-term employment

**"PPE Doesn't Fit Right"**:
- **Individual fitting sessions**: Work with each person to achieve proper fit
- **Multiple options**: Provide various brands/styles when possible
- **Custom solutions**: Special ordering for difficult-to-fit workers
- **Accommodation processes**: ADA considerations for workers with disabilities

# Emerging Technologies in Protective Equipment

The PPE industry continues to evolve with new materials, designs, and technologies that address traditional limitations while providing enhanced protection and user acceptance.

## Smart PPE and Wearable Technology
**Integrated Sensor Systems:**
- **Impact detection**: Hard hats with sensors that detect dangerous impacts
- **Environmental monitoring**: Real-time detection of gases, temperature, noise levels
- **Location tracking**: GPS integration for emergency response and accountability
- **Fatigue monitoring**: Biometric sensors that detect worker exhaustion

**Communication Integration:**
- **Bluetooth connectivity**: Wireless communication through hard hat systems
- **Noise cancellation**: Active systems that allow communication in noisy environments
- **Translation capabilities**: Real-time language translation for diverse crews
- **Emergency alerting**: Automatic distress calls based on sensor data

**Data Analytics Applications:**
- **Usage monitoring**: Track when and how PPE is used
- **Maintenance prediction**: Sensors indicate when replacement is needed
- **Compliance verification**: Automated documentation of PPE use
- **Performance optimization**: Data-driven improvements to PPE programs

## Advanced Materials and Design
**Next-Generation Materials:**
- **Graphene-enhanced fibers**: Ultra-lightweight with superior cut resistance
- **Phase-change materials**: Regulate temperature for thermal comfort

- **Antimicrobial treatments**: Prevent odor and bacterial growth
- **Self-healing materials**: Minor damage repairs automatically

**Ergonomic Innovations**:
- **3D scanning and printing**: Custom-fitted PPE based on individual body measurements
- **Flexible electronics**: Sensors and displays integrated into fabric
- **Adaptive systems**: PPE that adjusts automatically to environmental conditions
- **Modular designs**: Interchangeable components for different hazard combinations

**Sustainability Advances**:
- **Recyclable materials**: PPE designed for end-of-life material recovery
- **Biodegradable options**: Disposable PPE that breaks down safely
- **Extended durability**: Longer-lasting equipment reduces waste
- **Remanufacturing programs**: Professional restoration of worn PPE

## Implementation Considerations for New Technologies

**Cost-Benefit Analysis**:
- **Initial investment**: Higher upfront costs vs. traditional PPE
- **Operational savings**: Reduced injuries, improved compliance, maintenance efficiency
- **Technology lifecycle**: Obsolescence and upgrade considerations
- **Training requirements**: Additional worker and supervisor education needs

**Integration Challenges**:
- **Existing systems**: Compatibility with current safety programs
- **Data management**: Information collection, storage, and analysis capabilities

- **Privacy concerns**: Worker acceptance of monitoring technologies
- **Reliability requirements**: Technology must work in harsh construction environments

**Pilot Program Approach**:
1. **Select limited application**: Test new technology in controlled environment
2. **Measure performance**: Compare to traditional PPE effectiveness
3. **Gather user feedback**: Worker acceptance and usability assessment
4. **Refine implementation**: Address issues before full deployment
5. **Scale gradually**: Expand successful technologies systematically

# Case Study: Transforming PPE Culture at Summit Construction

## Background

Summit Construction, a mid-sized commercial contractor in Seattle, faced persistent challenges with PPE compliance despite having comprehensive policies and regular training programs. Their OSHA injury rates were 15% above industry average, with 60% of incidents involving inadequate or improperly used PPE.

The company's traditional approach focused on enforcement: safety inspections, disciplinary actions for non-compliance, and mandatory training sessions. However, this approach created an adversarial relationship between safety staff and field workers, with compliance being viewed as something imposed rather than embraced.

**The Challenge Assessment**

**Data Analysis Revealed**:
- PPE compliance rates varied dramatically between crews (45% to 85%)
- Highest injury rates occurred among experienced workers who "knew better"
- Workers frequently modified or removed PPE during tasks
- Equipment damage and loss rates were extremely high
- Training evaluations showed understanding but not behavior change

**Root Cause Investigation**:
1. **Comfort Issues**: Standard-issue PPE didn't accommodate diverse body types and preferences
2. **Task Interference**: PPE selection didn't consider specific job requirements
3. **Cultural Resistance**: Safety was seen as management priority, not worker priority
4. **Inadequate Involvement**: Workers had no input into PPE selection decisions
5. **Inconsistent Leadership**: Supervisors didn't consistently model or enforce PPE use

## The Transformation Strategy
**Phase 1: Worker Engagement and Assessment** (Months 1-2)
Summit formed PPE evaluation teams with representatives from each crew. These teams:
- Tested different brands and styles of PPE equipment
- Identified specific comfort and functionality issues
- Developed criteria for equipment selection based on actual use conditions
- Created feedback systems for ongoing equipment evaluation

**Phase 2: Customized Equipment Program** (Months 3-4) Based

on worker input, Summit implemented:
- **Individual fitting sessions** with multiple brand options
- **Task-specific PPE kits** designed for different types of work
- **Quality upgrade** to higher-end equipment with better comfort features
- **Personal issue system** where workers were assigned specific equipment

**Phase 3: Peer-Led Training Revolution** (Months 4-6) Traditional classroom training was replaced with:
- **Crew-based training sessions** led by respected workers
- **Hands-on demonstrations** using actual job site scenarios
- **Problem-solving workshops** where crews developed solutions to PPE challenges
- **Success story sharing** where workers discussed how PPE prevented their injuries

**Phase 4: Cultural Integration** (Months 6-12) PPE became integrated into company culture through:
- **Leadership modeling** with executives and supervisors consistently using PPE
- **Recognition programs** celebrating crews with excellent PPE compliance
- **Equipment care training** teaching workers to maintain and extend PPE life
- **Continuous improvement** with regular feedback and equipment updates

## Implementation Results
**Quantitative Improvements** (12-month comparison):
- PPE compliance rates increased from 67% to 94%
- Injury rates decreased by 40%
- PPE-related incidents decreased by 78%
- Equipment replacement costs decreased by 25% (due to better care)
- Training time per worker decreased by 30% (more effective methods)

**Qualitative Changes**:
- Worker satisfaction surveys showed 85% approval of new PPE program
- Supervisors reported easier enforcement due to voluntary compliance
- New workers adapted to PPE use more quickly due to positive peer influence
- Client feedback improved due to professional appearance and safety performance

## Key Success Factors

**Worker Ownership**: The most critical factor was involving workers in equipment selection and program design. When workers felt their input was valued and their comfort was prioritized, compliance became voluntary rather than forced.

**Quality Investment**: Upgrading to higher-quality, more comfortable equipment had immediate impact on usage rates. The additional cost was quickly offset by reduced injuries and replacement needs.

**Peer Leadership**: Training and enforcement by respected coworkers was far more effective than management-led programs. Workers trusted information from people who actually performed the work.

**Continuous Adaptation**: The program remained dynamic, with regular feedback loops and equipment updates based on field experience.

## Lessons for Safety Professionals

**Beyond Compliance Thinking**: The most successful PPE programs focus on creating conditions where workers want to use equipment properly, not just forcing compliance through rules and enforcement.

**Investment vs. Cost Mentality**: Higher-quality PPE that workers will actually use correctly is far more cost-effective than cheap equipment that sits unused or is used improperly.

**Human-Centered Design**: PPE programs must be designed around how people actually work, not how we think they should work. Comfort, convenience, and functionality drive behavior more than safety knowledge.

**Cultural Change Takes Time**: Sustainable improvements in PPE use require fundamental shifts in how safety is perceived and valued. This cultural change happens over months and years, not days and weeks.

---

# Chapter Summary

Personal Protective Equipment represents the final barrier between workers and workplace hazards. This chapter has equipped you with comprehensive understanding of:

**Strategic PPE Management**:
- Understanding PPE's role as last resort protection that remains essential
- Hazard-driven selection that matches equipment capabilities to actual risks
- Human factors considerations that determine real-world effectiveness

**Technical Competence**:
- Detailed selection criteria for all major PPE categories
- Proper use procedures that ensure equipment provides intended protection
- Maintenance and storage systems that extend equipment life and reliability

**Program Implementation**:
- Training strategies that create understanding and commitment, not just compliance

- Emerging technologies that enhance protection while addressing traditional limitations
- Cultural transformation approaches that make PPE use voluntary rather than forced

**Professional Development**:
- Case study analysis showing how theory translates to practice
- Understanding of PPE's integration with broader safety management systems
- Recognition of economic and human factors that influence program success

Remember that PPE success is measured not by compliance percentages or equipment purchases, but by the injuries prevented and lives protected. The most sophisticated equipment provides no protection if workers don't use it correctly, while simple equipment used properly can prevent catastrophic injuries.

As you advance in your safety career, you'll find that PPE management becomes a window into broader organizational culture and effectiveness. Companies that excel at PPE programs typically excel at safety overall, because the same factors that drive proper PPE use - worker engagement, management commitment, continuous improvement, and respect for human factors - drive success in all safety activities.

In our next chapter, we'll explore the major construction hazards that make PPE necessary. Your understanding of proper PPE selection and use will directly inform how you develop comprehensive protection strategies for fall hazards, electrical safety, excavation risks, and other life-threatening construction exposures.

## Key Takeaways

- **PPE is last resort, not first choice** - But when needed, it must be selected and used with precision
- **Hazard analysis drives selection** - Generic PPE solutions often fail to protect against specific risks
- **Comfort enables compliance** - Equipment that workers want to wear is infinitely more effective than equipment they're forced to wear
- **Training creates understanding** - Focus on why and how, not just what and when
- **Maintenance ensures reliability** - PPE that isn't properly maintained provides false security
- **Technology enhances capability** - But basic principles of selection, use, and maintenance remain

# CHAPTER 6: MAJOR CONSTRUCTION HAZARDS

*"In construction, the difference between a close call and a catastrophe is often measured in inches and seconds."*

---

Construction sites are inherently dangerous places where massive forces, hazardous materials, and complex operations converge in constantly changing environments. As a safety professional, your ability to recognize, assess, and control the major hazards that define construction work will determine not just your career success, but the lives and wellbeing of the workers you're sworn to protect.

This chapter examines the "Fatal Four" hazards that account for over 60% of construction fatalities - falls, electrocution, struck-by objects, and caught-in/between incidents - along with other major hazards that pose serious risks to construction workers. But we won't just catalog dangers; we'll provide you with the systematic approaches, proven strategies, and practical tools needed to prevent these hazards from claiming lives.

Understanding these hazards deeply means thinking like both an engineer and a detective. You'll learn to see the physics behind failures, the human factors that create vulnerabilities, and the systematic approaches that create robust protection. Most importantly, you'll develop the judgment to prioritize limited resources where they'll have the greatest impact on worker safety.

## Fall Protection Systems and Strategies

Falls represent the leading cause of construction fatalities, accounting for more than one-third of all deaths in the industry. But falls are also among the most preventable hazards when proper systems and strategies are implemented systematically.

### Understanding Fall Physics and Injury Mechanisms
**The Deadly Math of Falls:**
- **6-foot rule**: OSHA requires fall protection at 6 feet for most construction work

- **Physics reality**: Fatal injuries can occur from as little as 4 feet depending on landing surface
- **Force calculation**: A 200-pound worker falling 6 feet generates approximately 12,000 pounds of force at arrest

**Injury Patterns by Fall Type**:
- **Same-level falls**: Typically result in fractures, sprains, lacerations
- **Falls to lower level**: Often cause traumatic brain injuries, spinal injuries, multiple trauma
- **Falls into/onto objects**: Impalement, crushing injuries, internal trauma
- **Arrested falls**: Suspension trauma, harness-related injuries

**Critical Factors in Fall Severity**:
- **Fall distance**: Directly related to impact force
- **Landing surface**: Concrete vs. soil vs. water makes dramatic difference
- **Body position**: Head-first falls typically fatal, feet-first often survivable
- **Age and health**: Older workers suffer more severe injuries from identical falls

## The Hierarchy of Fall Protection

Following the hierarchy of controls, fall protection strategies should be implemented in order of effectiveness:

### Elimination: Designing Out Fall Hazards
**Ground-Level Assembly**:
- Prefabricate wall sections, roof trusses, and other components at ground level
- Use crane systems to position completed assemblies
- Design buildings to minimize work at height during construction

**Alternative Construction Methods**:

- **Precast concrete**: Reduces on-site work at height
- **Modular construction**: Complete sections built in controlled environments
- **Ground-up construction**: Techniques that eliminate elevated work platforms

**Example Application**: Instead of traditional stick-built framing requiring workers on roof peaks, use prefabricated roof trusses lifted into place by crane, with workers only needed for final connections from secure platforms.

## Engineering Controls: Physical Barriers
**Guardrail Systems** (OSHA 1926.502(b)):
**Design Requirements**:
- **Top rail**: 42 inches ± 3 inches above walking surface
- **Midrail**: Halfway between top rail and platform surface
- **Strength**: 200 pounds applied downward or outward on top rail
- **Openings**: No gap greater than 19 inches

**Installation Considerations**:
- **Post spacing**: Maximum 8 feet on center for lumber, 6 feet for metal
- **End connections**: Properly secured to structure, not just balanced
- **Gate systems**: Self-closing and self-latching when required
- **Toe boards**: Required when tools or materials could fall

**Safety Net Systems**:
**Applications**:
- Bridge construction over water or traffic
- High-rise construction for protection during steel erection
- Precast concrete operations
- Any situation where guardrails are not feasible

**Installation Standards**:
- **Maximum gap**: 6 inches between net and work surface
- **Border rope**: Minimum 5,000-pound breaking strength
- **Mesh size**: Maximum 36 square inches, minimum 150-pound breaking strength
- **Drop testing**: Required after installation and weekly thereafter

**Hole Covers**:
- **Load capacity**: Support twice the weight of employees, equipment, and materials
- **Marking**: Clearly identified as covers, not work surfaces
- **Securing**: Prevent displacement by wind, equipment, or personnel
- **Materials**: Plywood minimum ¾ inch thick, steel plate minimum ¼ inch

**Personal Fall Arrest Systems (PFAS)**

When elimination and engineering controls aren't feasible, personal fall arrest systems become critical protection.

**System Components**:
**Full Body Harness**:
- **D-ring placement**: Dorsal (back) for general use, chest for confined space rescue
- **Fit requirements**: Snug but not restrictive, allows full range of motion
- **Capacity**: Rated for user weight plus tools and equipment
- **Inspection**: Before each use for cuts, burns, chemical damage, excessive wear

**Connecting Devices**:
- **Shock-absorbing lanyards**: Reduce arrest force to maximum 1,800 pounds
- **Self-retracting lifelines**: Automatically adjust to

worker movement
- **Positioning devices**: Allow hands-free work while maintaining protection
- **Rope grabs**: Slide freely up, lock when loaded

**Anchorage Points**:
- **Strength requirement**: 5,000 pounds per attached worker, or engineered system with 2:1 safety factor
- **Location**: Above worker to minimize fall distance
- **Sharp edges**: Protect connecting devices from cutting or abrasion
- **Multiple users**: Reduce strength proportionally (3,000 pounds each for two workers)

**Critical Installation Factors**:

**Swing Fall Hazards**: Calculate potential pendulum motion if worker falls while attached to side-mounted anchor point. Swing radius can cause impact with structures or other hazards.

**Clearance Calculations**:
- **Free fall distance**: Distance worker falls before system begins to arrest
- **Deceleration distance**: Distance required for shock absorber to stop worker
- **Safety factor**: Additional distance to account for harness stretch, rope elongation
- **Total clearance**: Sum of all factors plus safety margin

**Example Calculation using shock absorbing lanyard:**
Worker on 6-foot lanyard with shock absorber
- Free Fall: 6 feet (lanyard length)
- Deceleration: 3.5 feet (shock absorber extionsion)
- Worker Height: 6 feet (average height)
- Harness stretch/D-Ring Shift: 1 foot
- Safety factor: 2 feet
- **Total clearance required:** 18.5 feet below work surface

**Work Positioning and Travel Restraint**

**Work Positioning Systems**: Allow workers to lean back against fall protection while using both hands for work tasks.

**Applications**:
- Ironwork connections
- Window installation from exterior
- Structural steel erection
- Tower climbing and maintenance

**Key Requirements**:
- Separate from fall arrest system (backup protection required)
- Limit fall potential to 2 feet maximum
- Inspect rigging before each use
- Position to prevent swing hazards

**Travel Restraint Systems**: Prevent worker from reaching fall hazard areas entirely.

**Design Principle**: System length prevents worker from getting close enough to edge to fall, even if they try.

**Advantages**:
- No fall arrest forces generated
- No clearance requirements below work surface
- Reduced inspection and maintenance requirements
- Worker cannot experience fall forces

## Specialized Fall Protection Applications
### Roofing Operations
**Low-slope roofs** (less than 4:12 pitch):
- **Warning line systems**: 6 feet from roof edge, combined with monitoring
- **Conventional fall protection**: Guardrails or personal fall arrest systems
- **Safety net systems**: Erected as close as possible to

work surface

**Steep roofs** (4:12 pitch or greater):
- **Personal fall arrest**: Required regardless of height
- **Guardrail systems**: Where structurally feasible
- **Safety nets**: Maximum 30 feet below work surface

**Built-up roofing considerations**:
- Hot asphalt creates additional burn hazards
- Equipment weight may exceed roof load capacity
- Weather conditions affect material handling and worker stability

## Steel Erection

**Controlled Decking Zones (CDZ)**: Special area where limited fall protection modifications are allowed during initial decking installation.

**Requirements**:
- Only for initial installation of metal decking
- Maximum 90 feet wide, 90 feet deep
- Safety nets or guardrails at leading edge
- Trained connector and puller only
- Crane operator trained in steel erection

**Connection work**:
- Fall arrest or positioning systems required
- Multiple tie-off points for complex connections
- Communication systems for coordinating with crane operators
- Weather restrictions for high-wind conditions

## Scaffolding Safety
**Supported Scaffolds**:
**Inspection Requirements**:
- **Daily**: Before each work shift
- **After incidents**: Weather events, impacts, modifications

- **Competent person**: Trained individual conducts inspections
- **Documentation**: Written records of inspections and corrective actions

**Fall Protection Integration**:
- **Guardrails**: Standard requirement for platforms 10 feet or higher
- **Personal fall arrest**: When guardrails not feasible
- **Planking**: Fully decked platforms, proper overlap and securing
- **Access**: Safe means of access (built-in ladders, stair towers)

**Suspended Scaffolds**:
- **Two-point suspension**: Most common type, requires fall arrest systems
- **Multi-point suspension**: Complex rigging requires engineered design
- **Daily inspection**: Hoisting equipment, rigging, platform components
- **Weather restrictions**: Wind speed limitations, precipitation concerns

# Electrical Safety and Lockout/Tagout

Electrical hazards in construction are unique because they're often invisible, can kill instantly, and exist in both obvious and hidden forms throughout construction sites. Electrical incidents typically result in the most severe injuries, with fatality rates far exceeding other construction hazards.

### Understanding Electrical Hazards in Construction
**Primary Electrical Hazards**:
**Shock and Electrocution**:
- **Contact with energized parts**: Direct touching of live wires, equipment
- **Ground faults**: Current flow through worker's body to ground

- **Arc faults**: Current flow through air, can cause serious burns
- **Secondary injuries**: Falls, burns from electrical contact

**Arc Flash and Arc Blast:**
- **Arc flash**: Intense heat and light from electrical arcing
- **Arc blast**: Pressure wave from rapidly expanding gases
- **Temperature**: Can exceed 35,000°F (four times hotter than sun's surface)
- **Pressure**: Blast can throw workers significant distances

**Electrical Fires:**
- **Ignition sources**: Overloaded circuits, damaged wiring, improper connections
- **Construction materials**: Many building materials are combustible
- **Evacuation challenges**: Construction sites often have limited egress routes

## Voltage Classifications and Safety Requirements
**Low Voltage (50-1000 volts):**
- **Most construction work**: 120V, 240V, 480V systems common
- **Still lethal**: Can cause ventricular fibrillation, respiratory paralysis
- **Protection methods**: GFCI, proper grounding, insulated tools
- **Common sources**: Temporary power, hand tools, lighting systems

**Medium Voltage (1000-35,000 volts):**
- **Utility connections**: Service entrances, large equipment
- **Increased hazard**: Greater likelihood of fatality from contact
- **Approach distances**: Minimum 10 feet for

unqualified persons
- **Special precautions**: Only qualified electricians, additional PPE

**High Voltage (over 35,000 volts)**:
- **Transmission lines**: Overhead power lines near construction sites
- **Extreme hazard**: Fatal contact can occur without direct touching
- **Clearance requirements**: Minimum distances based on voltage level
- **Equipment restrictions**: Crane operations, tall equipment limitations

## Ground Fault Circuit Interrupters (GFCI)

**How GFCIs Work**: Monitor electrical current flowing in circuit conductors. When imbalance is detected (indicating current leaking to ground), device trips circuit within 1/40th of a second.

**OSHA Requirements**:
- **All 120V outlets**: On construction sites must be GFCI protected
- **Temporary wiring**: Extension cords, portable equipment
- **Wet locations**: Any area where water contact is possible
- **Testing**: Monthly testing of GFCI devices required

**Types of GFCI Protection**:

**GFCI Outlets**:
- **Built-in protection**: Device integrated into outlet
- **Test/reset buttons**: Allow functional testing
- **Limitations**: Protects only downstream connections
- **Applications**: Permanent installations, specific location protection

**GFCI Circuit Breakers**:
- **Panel protection**: Protects entire circuit from electrical panel

- **Advantage**: Protects all outlets on circuit
- **Cost consideration**: More expensive than GFCI outlets
- **Maintenance**: Accessible location for testing and reset

**Portable GFCI Devices:**
- **Temporary protection**: Plug-in devices for extension cords
- **Flexibility**: Can be moved between locations
- **Durability**: Must withstand construction site conditions
- **Testing**: More frequent testing due to harsh environment

## Lockout/Tagout (LOTO) Procedures

Lockout/Tagout procedures ensure that equipment cannot be energized while workers are performing maintenance, repair, or construction activities.

**Energy Sources Requiring LOTO:**
- **Electrical**: Circuit breakers, disconnect switches, fuses
- **Pneumatic**: Compressed air systems, pneumatic tools
- **Hydraulic**: Hydraulic pumps, cylinders, accumulators
- **Mechanical**: Springs, rotating equipment, elevated components
- **Thermal**: Steam, hot water, chemical heat sources
- **Chemical**: Hazardous material flows, reactive chemicals

**LOTO Procedure Development:**
**Step 1: Equipment Survey**
- Identify all energy sources connected to equipment
- Locate all isolation points (switches, valves, breakers)
- Determine proper isolation procedures
- Identify stored energy that must be dissipated

**Step 2: Written Procedures**
- **Equipment identification**: Specific name, location, description
- **Energy sources**: All forms of energy present
- **Isolation methods**: Step-by-step shutdown procedures
- **Lockout devices**: Specific locks, tags, blocks required
- **Verification**: Testing procedures to confirm zero energy

**Step 3: Training Requirements**
- **Authorized employees**: Perform lockout procedures
- **Affected employees**: Work on or near equipment being serviced
- **Other employees**: May be in area during lockout activities

**LOTO Implementation Process:**
**Preparation Phase:**
1. **Notify affected workers**: Equipment will be shut down and locked out
2. **Identify energy sources**: Verify all energy sources documented
3. **Plan procedure**: Review written LOTO procedure
4. **Gather materials**: Locks, tags, testing equipment

**Isolation Phase:**
1. **Normal shutdown**: Follow equipment manufacturer's procedures
2. **Isolate energy sources**: Open switches, close valves, remove fuses
3. **Apply lockout devices**: Physical locks prevent re-energization
4. **Apply warning tags**: Information about lockout status and personnel

**Verification Phase:**
1. **Test isolation**: Attempt to operate equipment (should not function)
2. **Check meters**: Voltage testers, pressure gauges confirm zero energy
3. **Dissipate stored energy**: Bleed hydraulics, discharge capacitors
4. **Retest**: Confirm no energy present after dissipation

**Group Lockout Procedures**: When multiple workers are involved:
- **Each worker**: Applies individual lock to group lockbox
- **Supervisor responsibility**: Maintains master procedure and accountability
- **Shift changes**: Transfer procedures ensure continuity
- **Emergency removal**: Detailed procedures for unusual circumstances

## Working Near Overhead Power Lines

Power line contact is a leading cause of electrical fatalities in construction, particularly involving cranes, concrete pumps, and other tall equipment.

**Minimum Approach Distances:**
- **Up to 50 kV**: 10 feet minimum
- **Over 50 kV**: Add 4 inches for every 10 kV above 50 kV
- **Transmission lines**: May require much greater distances
- **Equipment in transit**: Same distances apply to mobile equipment

**Crane Operations Near Power Lines:**
**Pre-job Planning:**
- **Utility coordination**: Contact utility company before work begins
- **Line identification**: Voltage determination, ownership, switching possibilities
- **Alternative methods**: Can work be done from different location?
- **De-energizing**: Request temporary power shutdown if feasible

**Protective Measures:**
- **Spotters**: Dedicated personnel to watch clearances
- **Boom guards**: Physical barriers to prevent contact
- **Insulating barriers**: Temporary covers over power lines (utility installed)
- **Communication**: Clear signals between operator and spotters

**Emergency Procedures**: If equipment contacts power lines:
1. **Stay in cab**: Safest location if possible
2. **Call for help**: Emergency services and utility company
3. **Jump clear**: If cab becomes unsafe, jump without touching equipment and ground simultaneously
4. **Shuffle away**: Small steps keeping feet together until at least 35 feet away

## Temporary Electrical Systems

Construction sites require extensive temporary electrical systems that create unique hazards.

**Temporary Wiring Requirements:**
- **GFCI protection**: All 120V outlets and equipment
- **Grounding**: Equipment grounding conductors in all circuits
- **Overcurrent protection**: Proper breaker/fuse sizing
- **Weather protection**: Suitable for outdoor/wet

location use

**Extension Cord Safety**:
- **Three-wire cords**: Grounding conductor required
- **Proper rating**: Ampacity matching tool requirements
- **Condition inspection**: Daily checks for damage, proper connections
- **Routing**: Avoid traffic areas, overhead hazards, sharp edges

**Portable Generator Safety**:
- **Carbon monoxide**: Never operate in enclosed or partially enclosed areas
- **Grounding**: Proper grounding electrode system
- **GFCI protection**: Required for all outlets
- **Fuel handling**: Safe storage and handling procedures

---

# Excavation and Trenching Safety

Excavation work presents some of the most serious hazards in construction. Cave-ins can occur without warning, trapping workers under tons of soil with little chance of survival. The physics of soil pressure and the unpredictability of ground conditions make excavation safety both critical and complex.

## Soil Mechanics and Cave-in Physics
**Soil Pressure Calculations**:
- **Lateral pressure**: Increases with depth (approximately 35 pounds per square foot per foot of depth in average soil)
- **Surcharge loads**: Additional pressure from equipment, materials, traffic near excavation
- **Water effects**: Saturated soil can double lateral pressures
- **Dynamic loads**: Vibration from equipment can trigger sudden failures

**Cave-in Characteristics**:

- **Speed**: Can occur in seconds with no warning
- **Volume**: A cubic yard of soil weighs approximately 3,000 pounds
- **Survivability**: Workers buried in cave-ins have very low survival rates
- **Rescue complexity**: Cave-in rescue requires specialized equipment and techniques

## Soil Classification System

OSHA requires soil classification to determine appropriate protective systems. This classification must be performed by a competent person.

**Type A Soil** (Most Stable):
- **Characteristics**: Clay, cemented soil, hardpan
- **Cohesive strength**: 1.5 tons per square foot or greater
- **Conditions**: No fissures, dry conditions
- **Allowable slope**: 3/4:1 (53° from horizontal)
- **Restrictions**: Cannot be Type A if previously disturbed, subject to vibration, or has seepage

**Type B Soil** (Medium Stability):
- **Characteristics**: Silt, sandy loam, medium clay
- **Cohesive strength**: 0.5 to 1.5 tons per square foot
- **Conditions**: Fissured or subject to vibration
- **Allowable slope**: 1:1 (45° from horizontal)
- **Most common**: Majority of excavation work occurs in Type B soil

**Type C Soil** (Least Stable):
- **Characteristics**: Sand, gravel, loamy sand
- **Cohesive strength**: Less than 0.5 tons per square foot
- **Conditions**: Granular, submerged, subject to heavy vibration
- **Allowable slope**: 1.5:1 (34° from horizontal)
- **Special concerns**: Cannot be sloped safely in some conditions

**Field Testing Methods**:

**Visual Test:**
- **Soil composition**: Granular vs. cohesive characteristics
- **Layering**: Different soil types, rock layers
- **Water conditions**: Seepage, standing water, saturation
- **Cracking**: Tension cracks indicating instability

**Plasticity Test:**
- **Procedure**: Roll soil sample into thread 1/8 inch diameter
- **Type A indication**: Thread holds together, can be bent
- **Type B/C indication**: Thread crumbles, cannot maintain shape
- **Limitations**: Only applies to cohesive soils

**Thumb Penetration Test:**
- **Type A soil**: Thumb penetrates less than 1 inch
- **Type B soil**: Thumb penetrates 1-2 inches
- **Type C soil**: Thumb easily penetrates more than 2 inches
- **Considerations**: Hand strength varies, use consistently

## Protective Systems for Excavations
### Sloping Systems:
### Simple Slope:
- **Application**: Straightforward excavations in uniform soil
- **Angle**: Based on soil type classification
- **Limitations**: Requires significant space, may not be practical in urban areas
- **Maintenance**: Slopes can deteriorate due to weather, vibration

### Compound Slope:
- **Multiple benches**: Different slopes for different soil types

- **Transition zones**: Where soil types change within excavation
- **Design complexity**: Requires engineering analysis for unusual configurations

**Shoring Systems:**

**Timber Shoring:**
- **Components**: Wales, struts, uprights, plywood sheeting
- **Advantages**: Readily available materials, field modifications possible
- **Disadvantages**: Labor intensive, limited reuse, variable quality
- **Applications**: Small excavations, unusual shapes, emergency repairs

**Hydraulic Shoring:**
- **Components**: Aluminum rails, hydraulic struts, steel plates
- **Advantages**: Quick installation, adjustable, consistent quality
- **Installation**: Can be installed from outside excavation
- **Limitations**: Standard sizes may not fit all excavations

**Pneumatic Shoring:**
- **Mechanism**: Air pressure extends shores against excavation walls
- **Advantages**: Rapid deployment, no hydraulic fluid leaks
- **Applications**: Emergency response, temporary installations
- **Maintenance**: Air compressor requirements, pressure monitoring

**Trench Boxes (Shield Systems):**

**Design Principles:**
- **Protection**: Workers protected inside box, not outside

- **Installation**: Lowered into excavation as digging progresses
- **Movement**: Can be moved along trench as work advances
- **Sizing**: Must fit excavation dimensions and soil conditions

**Installation Procedures**:
1. **Excavate to maximum allowable unsupported depth** (typically 4 feet)
2. **Position box**: Center in excavation, level and plumb
3. **Continue excavation**: Inside and alongside box simultaneously
4. **Maintain clearance**: Maximum 2 feet between box and excavation wall
5. **Support box**: Prevent floating in groundwater conditions

**Safety Considerations**:
- **Entry/exit**: Safe means of access required
- **Clearances**: Workers must stay within protected area
- **Box condition**: Regular inspection for damage, deformation
- **Lifting**: Proper rigging when moving with excavator

## Excavation Hazards Beyond Cave-ins

**Hazardous Atmospheres**:
- **Oxygen deficiency**: Normal air contains 20.9% oxygen, hazardous below 19.5%
- **Toxic gases**: Hydrogen sulfide, carbon monoxide, methane
- **Flammable atmospheres**: Methane, gasoline vapors, other combustibles
- **Testing requirements**: Before entry and continuously during work

**Water Accumulation**:
- **Dewatering systems**: Pumps, well points, drainage
- **Equipment safety**: Electrical hazards with water present
- **Soil instability**: Water pressure reduces soil strength
- **Drowning hazard**: Rapid water accumulation can

trap workers

**Mobile Equipment Hazards:**
- **Struck-by incidents**: Excavators, dump trucks, compactors
- **Visibility**: Operators may not see workers in excavation
- **Traffic control**: Separating equipment from personnel
- **Communication**: Clear signals between equipment operators and ground workers

## Utility Location and Protection

**Call Before You Dig Requirements:**
- **811 notification**: Required 2-3 business days before excavation
- **Marking standards**: Color codes for different utility types
- **Mark duration**: Temporary marks require refresh for extended projects
- **Verification**: Confirm all utilities have been marked

**Hand Digging Requirements:**
- **Tolerance zone**: Within 18-24 inches of marked utilities (varies by state)
- **Excavation method**: Hand tools only, no mechanical equipment
- **Exposure procedures**: Careful uncovering to determine exact location
- **Support systems**: Protect exposed utilities from damage

**Utility Damage Prevention:**
- **Pre-excavation meeting**: Utility companies, contractors, inspectors
- **Damage procedures**: Immediate notification requirements
- **Emergency response**: Gas leaks, electrical contact, water main breaks
- **Documentation**: Photos, incident reports, regulatory notifications

# Crane and Heavy Equipment Operations

Crane operations represent some of the highest-risk activities in construction. The combination of massive weights, complex rigging, and coordination between multiple workers creates scenarios where small mistakes can have catastrophic consequences.

## Crane Safety Fundamentals

**Load Chart Understanding**: Every crane operation must stay within the manufacturer's rated capacity as defined by load charts.

**Variables Affecting Capacity**:
- **Boom length**: Longer boom reduces lifting capacity
- **Boom angle**: Lower angles reduce capacity significantly
- **Radius**: Distance from center of rotation to load
- **Counterweight**: Removable counterweight affects ratings
- **Track position**: Extended vs. retracted crawler tracks

**Load Chart Application**:
1. **Determine configuration**: Boom length, counterweight, track position
2. **Calculate radius**: Horizontal distance to load's center of gravity
3. **Find intersection**: Boom angle and radius on load chart
4. **Apply safety factors**: Never exceed 75% of chart capacity for personnel lifting
5. **Consider dynamics**: Swinging, hoisting accelerations reduce effective capacity

**Pre-Operation Inspections:**
**Daily Inspections** (by operator):
- **Visual inspection**: Structural components, wire rope, hooks
- **Functional testing**: All controls, safety devices, warning systems
- **Fluid levels**: Hydraulic, coolant, fuel, lubricants
- **Documentation**: Inspection checklist, deficiency reporting

**Periodic Inspections** (by qualified person):
- **Monthly**: Detailed examination of all safety-critical components
- **Annual**: Comprehensive inspection including non-destructive testing
- **After incidents**: Any incident involving crane or rigging failure
- **Certification**: Written reports, component replacement records

## Rigging Safety and Load Control
**Sling Selection and Inspection:**
**Wire Rope Slings:**
- **Construction**: 6x19, 6x37 classifications for different applications
- **Capacity**: Based on diameter, construction, sling angle
- **Inspection criteria**: Broken wires, kinks, bird caging, corrosion
- **Retirement criteria**: 10% wire breakage in lay length, severe kinking

**Chain Slings:**
- **Grades**: Grade 80, Grade 100 for overhead lifting
- **Capacity**: Stamped on master link, varies with sling configuration
- **Inspection**: Cracks, excessive wear, deformation,

missing identification
- **Heat damage**: Discoloration indicates overheating, requires retirement

**Synthetic Slings**:
- **Materials**: Nylon, polyester, polypropylene for different applications
- **Advantages**: Light weight, won't scratch delicate surfaces
- **Limitations**: Chemical sensitivity, temperature restrictions, UV degradation
- **Inspection**: Cuts, burns, chemical contamination, stitching damage

**Sling Angle Effects**: Understanding how sling angles affect load distribution is critical for safe rigging.
**Load Distribution**:
- **60° sling angle**: Each leg carries 58% of load weight
- **45° sling angle**: Each leg carries 71% of load weight
- **30° sling angle**: Each leg carries 100% of load weight
- **Rule**: Never use sling angles less than 45°

**Rigging Hardware**:
- **Shackles**: Properly sized, inspection for cracks and deformation
- **Load blocks**: Rated capacity, bearing condition, wire rope tracking
- **Hooks**: Latch operation, throat opening, load block attachment
- **Spreader beams**: Engineered lifting devices for wide loads

## Mobile Crane Operations
**Ground Conditions and Setup**:
- **Bearing capacity**: Soil must support crane plus maximum load
- **Outrigger setup**: Float size, blocking, level setup

- **Slope limitations**: Maximum allowable grade for operation
- **Overhead clearances**: Power lines, structures, other cranes

**Operating Procedures:**
**Load Handling:**
1. **Plan the lift**: Review load weight, dimensions, rigging points
2. **Test lift**: Raise load slightly to verify balance and rigging
3. **Communication**: Clear signals between operator and signal person
4. **Smooth operation**: Avoid sudden movements, load swinging
5. **Landing**: Control load placement, maintain rigging tension

**Multi-Crane Lifts:**
- **Engineering analysis**: Load distribution, crane capacities, coordination
- **Lift director**: Qualified person to coordinate multiple operators
- **Communication systems**: Clear, redundant communication between all parties
- **Contingency planning**: Procedures if one crane fails during lift

## Heavy Equipment Safety
**Excavator Safety:**
**Stability Factors:**
- **Track positioning**: Proper track spread for working conditions
- **Counterweight**: Maintain counterweight toward heavy loads
- **Operating radius**: Stay within stability limits for digging depth
- **Ground conditions**: Soft soil, slopes, excavation

edges affect stability

**Struck-By Prevention:**
- **Swing radius**: Establish and maintain clear swing zones
- **Visibility**: Spotters for blind areas, backup alarms
- **Communication**: Hand signals, radio systems
- **Traffic control**: Separate equipment operations from pedestrian areas

**Bulldozer and Scraper Operations:**
- **Rollover protection**: ROPS/FOPS systems required and maintained
- **Slope limitations**: Maximum safe operating angles
- **Visibility**: Clear sight lines, spotter assistance
- **Maintenance access**: Safe procedures for track and blade maintenance

**Concrete Pump Safety:**
- **Setup stability**: Outrigger placement, ground bearing capacity
- **Boom operation**: Avoid power lines, maintain clearances
- **Pressure systems**: High-pressure hydraulics, proper lockout procedures
- **Concrete delivery**: Coordination with ready-mix trucks, placement crews

## Chemical and Respiratory Hazards

Construction workers face exposure to numerous chemical hazards through cutting, welding, painting, and material handling activities. Many construction materials contain hazardous substances that require specific control measures.

### Common Construction Chemical Hazards
**Silica exposure** occurs during cutting, grinding, or drilling concrete, stone, or masonry materials. Crystalline silica particles can cause silicosis, lung cancer, and other serious

health effects. New OSHA standards require specific control measures for silica-generating activities.

**Asbestos hazards** persist in renovation and demolition work involving older buildings. Asbestos-containing materials require specialized removal procedures and trained personnel. Even small-scale disturbance can create significant exposure risks.

**Lead exposure** commonly occurs during renovation of structures built before 1978. Lead-based paint removal requires specific work practices, containment measures, and worker protection. The EPA's Renovation, Repair, and Painting (RRP) Rule establishes requirements for lead-safe work practices.

**Welding fumes** contain various metal oxides and other hazardous substances. Fume composition depends on base metals, consumables, and coatings. Adequate ventilation and respiratory protection prevent overexposure to these materials.

### Respiratory Protection Programs
**Hazard assessment** identifies airborne contaminants and determines appropriate protection levels. Air monitoring may be necessary to quantify exposure levels and select proper equipment.

**Respirator selection** must match hazard types and concentrations. Air-purifying respirators work for many construction applications, but supplied-air systems may be necessary for high-concentration or oxygen-deficient environments.

**Medical evaluation** ensures workers can safely use respiratory protection equipment. Certain medical conditions may prevent safe respirator use or require specific accommodation.

**Fit testing** verifies that tight-fitting respirators provide adequate face seals. Annual testing and additional testing after significant facial changes ensure continued protection effectiveness.

**Training and maintenance** programs ensure proper respirator use and care. Workers must understand equipment limitations, inspection requirements, and storage procedures.

## Chemical Safety Program Implementation

**Material identification** requires understanding of all chemicals present on construction sites. Safety data sheets (SDSs) provide essential hazard information and control recommendations.

**Exposure controls** follow the hierarchy of controls, emphasizing elimination and substitutions when possible. Engineering controls like ventilation systems provide preferred protection methods over personal protective equipment.

**Emergency procedures** address potential chemical releases, exposures, and injuries. Emergency eyewash and shower facilities may be required depending on chemical hazards present.

## Integration and Practical Application

Managing major construction hazards requires integrated approaches that consider interaction between different hazard types. A comprehensive safety program addresses all significant hazards while recognizing their interconnected nature.

**Hazard assessment processes** must be ongoing and dynamic. Construction sites change rapidly, creating new hazards and eliminating others. Regular reassessment ensures that control measures remain appropriate and effective.

**Worker training programs** should address multiple hazard types and their interactions. Cross training helps workers recognize hazards outside their primary work areas and understand how their activities might affect others.

**Coordination between trades** prevents one group's work from creating hazards for others. Hot work permits, confined space procedures, and lift plans require input from multiple specialties to ensure comprehensive hazard control.

Your role as a safety professional involves not just understanding individual hazards, but developing systems that address the complex, dynamic environment of construction work. This requires technical knowledge, practical experience, and the ability to communicate effectively with diverse groups of workers and managers.

The next chapter will explore how to develop essential skills for safety professionals, building on this foundation of hazard knowledge to create practical competencies that will serve you throughout your career.

# CHAPTER 7: EDUCATIONAL PATHWAYS AND CERTIFICATIONS

*"Education is the most powerful weapon which you can use to change the world - and in construction safety, it's the weapon you use to save lives."*

When Sarah Martinez first stepped onto a construction site as a recent college graduate with a degree in occupational safety, she quickly realized that her formal education was just the beginning. The real learning - understanding how theory translated into practice, how to communicate with seasoned workers, and how to navigate the complex web of regulations - happened through a combination of continued education, professional certifications, and hands-on experience.

Like Sarah, every aspiring construction safety professional faces critical decisions about their educational path. Should you pursue a four-year degree, or can you succeed with specialized certificates? Which certifications carry the most weight with employers? How do you balance learning with earning a living? This chapter will guide you through these decisions and help you build an educational foundation that will serve your entire career.

# The Foundation: Formal Education Options

### Four-Year Degree Programs

A bachelor's degree in occupational safety and health, industrial hygiene, or a related field provides the broadest foundation for a construction safety career. These programs typically cover:

**Core Curriculum Areas:**
- Safety management principles and theory
- Industrial hygiene and environmental health
- Risk assessment and hazard analysis
- Safety regulations and legal compliance
- Statistics and data analysis
- Psychology and human factors
- Business and management principles
- Technical writing and communication

**Advantages of a Four-Year Degree:**
- Comprehensive theoretical foundation
- Higher starting salaries (typically $5,000-$15,000 more annually)
- Better long-term advancement opportunities
- Eligibility for management training programs
- Stronger analytical and research skills
- Network of academic and professional contacts

**Popular Degree Programs:**
- Occupational Safety and Health
- Industrial Hygiene

- Construction Management with Safety Emphasis
- Environmental Health and Safety
- Fire Protection Engineering
- Risk Management and Insurance

**Top Universities for Safety Programs:**
- University of Wisconsin-Whitewater
- Indiana University of Pennsylvania
- Murray State University
- Rochester Institute of Technology
- Texas A&M University
- Colorado State University
- Columbia Southern University

## Two-Year Associate Degree Programs

Associate degrees in occupational safety or related fields offer a faster path to employment while still providing solid foundational knowledge.

**Typical Program Content:**
- OSHA regulations and standards
- Hazard recognition and control
- Safety program development
- Incident investigation
- Basic industrial hygiene
- Construction safety fundamentals
- Emergency response planning

**Benefits of Associate Degrees:**
- Shorter time to employment (18-24 months)
- Lower educational costs
- Practical, hands-on focus
- Often include internship opportunities
- Good stepping stone to bachelor's degree
- Strong job placement rates

## Certificate Programs and Professional Training

Professional certificate programs offer focused, intensive training in specific areas of construction safety. These are ideal for career changers or those seeking to specialize quickly.

**Types of Certificate Programs:**

**OSHA Training Institute (OTI) Programs:**
- 30-Hour Construction Outreach Training
- 500/501 Trainer Courses
- Specialized courses in scaffolding, fall protection, cranes, etc.

**University-Based Certificate Programs:**
- Construction Safety Management
- Industrial Hygiene Fundamentals
- Safety Leadership and Management
- Environmental Compliance

**Professional Organization Certificates:**
- National Safety Council courses
- American Society of Safety Professionals (ASSP) learning modules
- Construction Industry Institute (CII) programs

# Professional Certifications: Your Credential Portfolio

Professional certifications demonstrate expertise, commitment to the field, and adherence to professional standards. They're often required for advancement and can significantly impact earning potential.

## The Big Four: CSP, SMP, ASP, and CHST
### Associate Safety Professional (ASP)
- **Eligibility:** Bachelor's degree in any field OR associate degree with 2 years safety experience
- **Exam:** 200 multiple-choice questions covering safety fundamentals
- **Best for:** Entry-level to mid-level professionals
- **Value:** Demonstrates foundational knowledge, stepping stone to CSP

### Certified Safety Professional (CSP)
- **Eligibility:** ASP certification plus 4 years professional safety experience
- **Exam:** 200 questions focusing on advanced safety management
- **Best for:** Senior-level professionals and managers
- **Value:** Gold standard certification, significant salary impact ($10,000-$20,000 increase)

### Construction Health and Safety Technician (CHST)
- **Eligibility:** High school diploma plus 3 years construction safety experience
- **Exam:** Construction-specific safety knowledge and applications
- **Best for:** Construction safety specialists and technicians
- **Value:** Industry-specific credibility, practical focus

### Safety Management Professional (SMP)
- **Eligibility:** Bachelor's degree plus 3 years safety management experience OR 7 years safety management experience
- **Exam:** Advanced safety management principles, leadership, and program development
- **Best for:** Safety managers and directors focused on management excellence

- **Value:** Demonstrates advanced management competency, leadership focus

## Specialized Construction Certifications
### Certified Crane Operator (CCO)
- National Commission for the Certification of Crane Operators
- Required in many jurisdictions
- Specific to crane types and capacities

### Certified Excavation Competent Person
- OSHA-required for excavation supervision
- Various providers offer certification
- Critical for trenching and excavation work

### Fall Protection Competent Person
- Required for fall protection program oversight
- Industry-specific training programs available
- High demand in construction industry

### Scaffold Competent Person
- OSHA requirement for scaffold erection and inspection
- Specialized training for different scaffold types
- Essential for high-rise construction projects

## International Certifications
### NEBOSH (National Examination Board in Occupational Safety and Health)
- International General Certificate
- Construction Certificate
- Recognized globally, especially valuable for international work

### IOSH (Institution of Occupational Safety and Health)
- Managing Safely
- Working Safely
- Strong international recognition

# Building Your Professional Development Plan

Creating a strategic approach to your education and certification journey is crucial for career success. Here's how to develop an effective plan:

## Step 1: Assess Your Current Position
**Career Stage Assessment:**
- Entry-level: Focus on foundational education and basic certifications
- Mid-career: Target specialized certifications and advanced degrees
- Senior-level: Consider doctoral studies or advanced management programs

**Skills Gap Analysis:**
- Technical knowledge areas needing improvement
- Communication and leadership skills
- Regulatory knowledge gaps
- Industry-specific expertise needs

## Step 2: Set Clear Goals
**Short-term Goals (1-2 years):**
- Complete specific training programs
- Obtain entry-level certifications
- Gain particular work experiences

**Medium-term Goals (3-5 years):**
- Achieve major professional certifications
- Complete degree requirements
- Develop specialization areas

**Long-term Goals (5+ years):**
- Advanced certifications and degrees
- Leadership development programs

- Teaching or consulting capabilities

## Step 3: Create Your Learning Timeline
**Sample 5-Year Development Plan:**
**Year 1:**
- Complete OSHA 30-Hour Construction
- Enroll in certificate program or degree
- Join professional association

**Year 2:**
- Obtain ASP certification
- Complete specialized training (fall protection, scaffolding)
- Attend industry conference

**Year 3:**
- Finish degree requirements
- Gain required experience for advanced certifications
- Develop mentor relationships

**Year 4:**
- Pursue CSP or CHST certification
- Complete leadership development program
- Begin specialization training

**Year 5:**
- Achieve advanced certification
- Consider graduate degree or specialized master's
- Begin mentoring others

# Continuing Education Requirements

Most professional certifications require ongoing education to maintain credentials. Understanding these requirements helps you plan effectively:

## Certification Maintenance Requirements
**ASP/CSP/SMP Recertification:**

- 30 continuing education points every 3 years
- Points earned through courses, conferences, writing, teaching
- Professional development activities must be safety-related

**CHST Recertification:**
- 40 contact hours every 4 years
- Construction safety-specific education required
- Volunteer activities and professional involvement count

**OSHA Trainer Cards:**
- No formal requirements but recommended annual updates
- New regulations and standards updates essential
- Best practice is continuous learning

## Strategies for Meeting CE Requirements
**Efficient Learning Approaches:**
- Choose courses that count for multiple certifications
- Attend conferences that offer CE credits
- Participate in webinars and online learning
- Engage in professional writing and speaking

**Cost-Effective Options:**
- Professional association member discounts
- Employer-sponsored training programs
- Online courses and webinars
- University continuing education programs

# Financing Your Education

Education and certification costs can be significant, but various funding options are available:

## Employer Sponsorship
**Negotiating Educational Support:**

- Link education to business needs
- Propose cost-sharing arrangements
- Commit to staying with company post-education
- Document expected ROI from training

**Common Employer Benefits:**
- Tuition reimbursement programs
- Conference attendance funding
- Certification exam fee payment
- Paid time off for study and exams

## Financial Aid and Scholarships
**Safety-Specific Scholarships:**
- ASSP Foundation scholarships
- NSC scholarship programs
- University-specific safety scholarships
- Industry association awards

**General Financial Aid:**
- Federal grants and loans
- State education programs
- Veteran's benefits
- Employer tuition assistance

## Self-Funding Strategies
**Budget Planning:**
- Create dedicated education savings account
- Plan certification timeline around finances
- Take advantage of early-bird pricing
- Consider payment plans when available

# Choosing the Right Educational Path

Selecting the best educational approach depends on your current situation, career goals, and learning style:

## For Career Changers
**Recommended Path:**
1. Start with OSHA 30-Hour Construction

2. Complete professional certificate program
3. Gain entry-level experience
4. Pursue ASP certification
5. Consider degree completion while working

**Timeline:** 2-3 years to establish credibility

### For Recent High School Graduates
**Recommended Path:**
1. Pursue bachelor's degree in safety or related field
2. Complete internships during school
3. Obtain ASP certification upon graduation
4. Focus on gaining diverse experience
5. Work toward CSP after required experience

**Timeline:** 4-6 years to professional-level position

### For Experienced Construction Workers
**Recommended Path:**
1. Complete OSHA trainer certification
2. Pursue CHST certification
3. Develop specialized expertise areas
4. Consider degree completion part-time
5. Transition gradually to safety role

**Timeline:** 1-2 years to safety position

# The Value of Continuous Learning

The construction industry continuously evolves, with new technologies, regulations, and best practices emerging regularly. Successful safety professionals commit to lifelong learning:

## Staying Current
**Industry Changes to Monitor:**
- New OSHA regulations and interpretations
- Emerging construction technologies
- Industry best practices and innovations
- Legal developments and case law
- Global safety trends and standards

**Learning Resources:**
- Professional journals and publications
- Industry websites and blogs
- Professional association resources
- Government agency updates
- Vendor and manufacturer training

## Building Expertise
**Developing Specialization:**
- Choose focus areas based on interest and opportunity
- Become the go-to expert in specific areas
- Contribute to industry knowledge through writing and speaking
- Mentor others in your specialty areas

**Example Specialization Areas:**
- Crane and rigging safety
- Fall protection systems
- Electrical safety in construction
- Excavation and trenching
- Green building safety
- International construction projects

# Making Your Educational Investment Pay Off

Education and certification represent significant investments of time and money. Maximizing the return requires strategic thinking:

## Career Advancement Strategies
**Leveraging New Credentials:**
- Update resume and LinkedIn profile immediately
- Inform current employer of new qualifications
- Apply for positions requiring new credentials
- Negotiate salary increases based on additional value

**Building Professional Reputation:**
- Share knowledge through presentations and articles
- Volunteer for challenging assignments
- Participate in professional committees
- Mentor junior professionals

## Measuring ROI
**Quantifiable Returns:**
- Salary increases from certifications
- Promotion opportunities
- Job security and employability
- Consulting and side income potential

**Intangible Benefits:**
- Professional confidence and credibility
- Expanded professional network
- Personal satisfaction and achievement
- Contribution to worker safety and lives saved

# Action Steps for Chapter 7
1. **Assess your current education and identify gaps**
2. **Research degree and certificate programs that fit your situation**
3. **Create a 5-year professional development plan**
4. **Set up a dedicated education savings account**
5. **Join a professional association for networking and resources**

6. **Schedule your first certification exam**
7. **Find a mentor in your desired specialization area**

## Key Takeaways

- Education is an investment that pays dividends throughout your career
- Combine formal education with professional certifications for maximum impact
- Create a strategic development plan aligned with your career goals
- Take advantage of employer sponsorship and scholarship opportunities
- Commit to continuous learning to stay current and competitive
- Specialize in areas that match your interests and market demand

The educational path you choose will shape your entire career in construction safety. Whether you pursue a traditional degree, professional certifications, or a combination of both, the key is to start now and maintain momentum. Every course completed, every certification earned, and every new skill developed brings you closer to your goal of becoming a construction safety professional who truly makes a difference.

Remember Sarah Martinez from the beginning of this chapter? Five years after starting her career, she had completed her CSP certification, specialized in crane safety, and was leading safety programs for major construction projects. Her commitment to continuous learning not only advanced her career but also contributed to a 40% reduction in accidents on her projects. Your educational journey can have the same transformative impact - on your career and on the lives of the workers you'll protect.

# CHAPTER 8: GAINING PRACTICAL EXPERIENCE

*"You can read about safety all day long, but until you've stood on a construction site at 6 AM watching crews gear up for another day of dangerous work, you don't really understand what we do."*

Mike Thompson learned this lesson the hard way. Fresh out of college with a degree in occupational safety and a head full of theoretical knowledge, he walked onto his first construction site confident he could immediately make a difference. Within his first week, he'd made three rookie mistakes: suggesting a safety procedure that would have doubled the project timeline, using technical jargon that confused experienced workers, and failing to recognize a serious electrical hazard that a journeyman electrician had to point out to him.

"That electrician probably saved my career," Mike reflects now, fifteen years later as a senior safety manager. "He didn't embarrass me in front of the crew, but he pulled me aside and said, 'Son, you've got the book knowledge, but you need to learn how things really work out here.' That conversation changed everything for me."

Mike's story illustrates a fundamental truth about construction safety careers: there's no substitute for hands-on experience. While education provides the foundation, practical experience builds the expertise, credibility, and judgment that separate effective safety professionals from those who struggle to make an impact. This chapter will guide you through the various pathways to gain that crucial experience and help you avoid the common pitfalls that can derail promising careers.

# Entry-Level Positions: Your Gateway to the Field

The construction safety field offers multiple entry points, each with distinct advantages and challenges. Understanding these options helps you choose the path that best fits your background and career goals.

### Safety Technician/Assistant

**Role Overview:** Safety technicians work under the supervision of experienced safety professionals, handling routine tasks while learning the ropes of construction safety management.

**Typical Responsibilities:**
- Conducting safety inspections and documenting findings
- Assisting with incident investigations
- Maintaining safety records and documentation
- Delivering toolbox talks and basic safety training
- Monitoring PPE compliance
- Supporting safety program implementation

**Skills You'll Develop:**
- Hazard recognition and documentation
- Basic investigation techniques
- Communication with construction workers
- Understanding of safety regulations
- Report writing and record keeping

**Entry Requirements:**
- High school diploma or equivalent
- OSHA 30-Hour Construction training preferred
- Basic computer skills
- Willingness to work in outdoor construction environments

**Salary Range:** $35,000 - $50,000 annually
**Career Progression:** Safety coordinator → Safety specialist → Safety manager

## Construction Safety Coordinator

**Role Overview:** Safety coordinators typically work on specific projects or with particular contractors, implementing and monitoring safety programs at the site level.

**Typical Responsibilities:**
- Developing and implementing site-specific safety plans
- Conducting pre-task safety meetings
- Performing safety audits and inspections
- Coordinating with subcontractors on safety requirements
- Managing safety documentation and reporting
- Investigating incidents and near-misses

**Skills You'll Develop:**
- Project-level safety program management
- Multi-contractor coordination
- Safety plan development

- Client and stakeholder communication
- Problem-solving under pressure

**Entry Requirements:**
- Associate degree or relevant certificates preferred
- OSHA 30-Hour Construction training
- 1-2 years related experience or strong internship background
- Strong communication and organizational skills

**Salary Range:** $45,000 - $65,000 annually

**Career Progression:** Senior safety coordinator → Safety manager → Regional safety director

## Environmental Health and Safety (EHS) Specialist

**Role Overview:** EHS specialists work for large construction companies or general contractors, focusing on both safety and environmental compliance across multiple projects.

**Typical Responsibilities:**
- Developing company-wide safety policies and procedures
- Conducting safety training programs
- Performing comprehensive safety audits
- Managing environmental compliance issues
- Analyzing safety data and trends
- Supporting business development with safety expertise

**Skills You'll Develop:**
- Multi-site safety program management
- Environmental regulations knowledge
- Data analysis and trending
- Policy development and implementation
- Training program design and delivery

**Entry Requirements:**
- Bachelor's degree in safety, environmental science, or related field
- ASP certification preferred
- Strong analytical and communication skills
- Understanding of environmental regulations

**Salary Range:** $55,000 - $75,000 annually

**Career Progression:** Senior EHS specialist → EHS manager → Corporate safety director

## The Power of Internships

Internships provide invaluable opportunities to gain experience while still in school or transitioning careers. They offer a low-risk way for employers to evaluate potential hires and for students to explore different aspects of construction safety.

### Types of Internship Opportunities
**General Contractor Internships:**
- Work directly on construction projects
- Exposure to diverse trades and hazards
- Experience with project lifecycle safety management
- Direct interaction with construction crews

**Engineering/Consulting Firm Internships:**
- Focus on safety program development
- Client interaction and project management
- Regulatory compliance and documentation
- Professional office environment experience

**Insurance Company Internships:**
- Risk assessment and loss control
- Claims investigation and analysis
- Client consultation and training

- Business perspective on safety investment

**Government Agency Internships:**
- Regulatory enforcement experience
- Compliance inspection procedures
- Public sector safety initiatives
- Policy development and implementation

## Maximizing Your Internship Experience
**Before You Start:**
- Research the company and their safety challenges
- Review relevant regulations and standards
- Prepare thoughtful questions about the industry
- Set clear learning objectives with your supervisor

**During Your Internship:**
- Volunteer for challenging assignments
- Ask questions and seek feedback regularly
- Network with professionals across the organization
- Document your experiences and learning
- Maintain a professional attitude and appearance

**After Your Internship:**
- Send thank-you notes to supervisors and mentors
- Stay in touch with professional contacts
- Update your resume with specific accomplishments
- Request LinkedIn recommendations
- Use the experience to refine your career goals

## Finding Internship Opportunities
**University Career Services:**
- Partner with career counselors to identify opportunities
- Attend career fairs and networking events
- Leverage alumni networks in the construction industry
- Participate in industry-specific job boards

**Professional Organizations:**

- ASSP student chapters often have internship programs
- AGC (Associated General Contractors) local chapters
- ABC (Associated Builders and Contractors) opportunities
- National Safety Council internship listings

**Direct Company Outreach:**
- Research major construction companies in your area
- Contact safety directors directly with internship proposals
- Attend industry conferences and networking events
- Use LinkedIn to connect with safety professionals

# Apprenticeship Programs: Learning While Earning

Traditional apprenticeships in construction trades can provide valuable safety experience, even if safety isn't the primary focus. Many successful safety professionals started as tradespeople, bringing credibility and practical understanding to their safety roles.

## Construction Trade Apprenticeships
### Electrical Apprenticeships:
- 4-year programs combining classroom and on-the-job training
- Strong focus on electrical safety and OSHA compliance
- Excellent foundation for electrical safety specialization
- High demand for electrical safety expertise in construction

### Carpentry Apprenticeships:
- Comprehensive exposure to fall protection systems
- Understanding of structural safety considerations
- Tool safety and material handling experience

- Foundation for general construction safety roles

**Ironworker Apprenticeships:**
- Intensive fall protection and height safety training
- Crane and rigging safety exposure
- High-risk work environment experience
- Excellent preparation for specialty safety roles

**Plumbing/Pipefitting Apprenticeships:**
- Confined space and excavation safety experience
- Chemical and respiratory hazard exposure
- Understanding of mechanical safety systems
- Good foundation for industrial safety careers

## Safety-Specific Apprenticeship Programs

Some progressive companies and unions have developed apprenticeship programs specifically for safety professionals:

**Program Features:**
- Combination of classroom instruction and field experience
- Mentorship from experienced safety professionals
- Rotational assignments across different project types
- Structured progression with increasing responsibility
- Paid positions with benefits and advancement opportunities

**Participating Organizations:**
- Large general contractors (Turner, Skanska, Bechtel)
- Specialty contractors with safety focus
- International unions with safety initiatives
- Government agencies and military contractors

## Creating Your Own Apprenticeship

If formal apprenticeship programs aren't available in your area, you can create informal apprenticeship relationships:

**Steps to Establish Mentorship:**
1. Identify experienced safety professionals in your network
2. Approach them with a specific learning proposal
3. Offer value in exchange for mentorship (research assistance, administrative support)
4. Set clear expectations and meeting schedules
5. Be respectful of their time and expertise
6. Document and share your learning progress

# Volunteering: Building Experience and Networks

Volunteer opportunities provide excellent ways to gain experience, demonstrate commitment, and build professional networks while contributing to worthy causes.

## Professional Organization Volunteering
### American Society of Safety Professionals (ASSP):
- Committee participation at local and national levels
- Conference planning and presentation opportunities
- Professional development program assistance
- Student chapter mentoring

### National Safety Council (NSC):
- Safety training program development
- Community safety initiatives
- Research project assistance
- Public awareness campaigns

### Construction Industry Organizations:
- AGC safety committee participation
- ABC safety training programs
- Specialty contractor association initiatives
- Industry conference planning

## Community Safety Programs
### Habitat for Humanity:
- Volunteer safety coordinator roles
- Training volunteer workers on safety procedures
- Implementing safety programs for construction projects
- Demonstrating safety leadership in community service

### Disaster Relief Organizations:
- Emergency response safety coordination
- Volunteer safety training programs
- Construction safety during relief efforts
- Experience with temporary and emergency construction

### Educational Institutions:
- Guest lecturing at universities and technical schools
- Developing safety curriculum and training materials
- Mentoring students in safety programs
- Participating in career development programs

## Benefits of Volunteer Experience
### Professional Development:
- Leadership experience in safety roles
- Public speaking and presentation skills
- Program development and implementation
- Cross-industry safety knowledge

### Network Building:
- Connections with industry professionals
- Exposure to different company cultures
- Mentorship opportunities
- Job referral networks

### Resume Enhancement:
- Demonstrates initiative and commitment
- Shows leadership and volunteer spirit
- Provides concrete examples of safety impact

- Differentiates you from other candidates

# Learning from Mentors and Industry Veterans

Mentorship is one of the most powerful tools for career development in construction safety. The right mentor can accelerate your learning, help you avoid common mistakes, and open doors to opportunities you might never have discovered on your own.

## Finding the Right Mentor
**Characteristics of Effective Mentors:**
- Extensive experience in construction safety
- Strong reputation and professional standing
- Willingness to share knowledge and connections
- Complementary skills to your development needs
- Commitment to your professional growth

**Where to Find Mentors:**
- Current workplace supervisors and colleagues
- Professional organization activities and events
- Industry conferences and networking events
- Alumni networks from your educational institutions
- LinkedIn and other professional networking platforms

## Types of Mentoring Relationships
**Formal Mentoring Programs:**
- Structured programs through professional organizations
- Company-sponsored mentorship initiatives
- University alumni mentoring networks
- Industry-specific mentoring programs

**Informal Mentoring Relationships:**
- Natural relationships that develop through work

- Connections made at professional events
- Referrals from mutual professional contacts
- Relationships built through volunteer activities

**Peer Mentoring:**
- Mutual mentoring with professionals at similar levels
- Study groups for certification preparation
- Professional development partnerships
- Industry networking circles

## Maximizing Mentoring Relationships

**As a Mentee:**
- Come prepared with specific questions and goals
- Respect your mentor's time and schedule
- Follow through on commitments and suggestions
- Share your progress and challenges honestly
- Express appreciation for their guidance and support

**Setting Expectations:**
- Define the scope and duration of the relationship
- Establish meeting frequency and communication methods
- Clarify what you hope to learn and achieve
- Understand what you can offer in return
- Set boundaries and professional guidelines

**Common Mentoring Topics:**
- Career planning and advancement strategies
- Technical knowledge and skill development
- Industry trends and future opportunities
- Professional networking and relationship building
- Work-life balance and career sustainability

# Building Diverse Experience

The most successful construction safety professionals have broad experience across different types of projects, companies, and roles. This diversity provides deeper understanding of the industry and greater career flexibility.

## Project Type Diversity
**Commercial Construction:**
- Office buildings, retail centers, hotels
- Focus on schedule-driven safety management
- Coordination with multiple trades and subcontractors
- Public safety considerations

**Industrial Construction:**
- Manufacturing facilities, power plants, refineries
- Complex safety systems and procedures
- Hazardous materials and processes
- Long-term project safety planning

**Infrastructure Projects:**
- Roads, bridges, utilities, airports
- Public works safety requirements
- Environmental and community considerations
- Government contract compliance

**Residential Construction:**
- Single-family homes, apartments, condominiums
- Small crew safety management
- Cost-conscious safety solutions
- Local code compliance

## Company Size and Culture Experience
**Large General Contractors:**
- Comprehensive safety programs and resources
- Multi-site project management
- Corporate safety policies and procedures
- Advanced safety technology and systems

**Specialty Contractors:**
- Deep expertise in specific trades
- Specialized safety knowledge and techniques
- Close-knit team environments
- Niche market understanding

**Small Construction Companies:**
- Hands-on, flexible safety approaches
- Direct owner/operator relationships
- Resource-constrained safety programs
- Entrepreneurial problem-solving

### Geographic and Regulatory Diversity
**Different Regional Markets:**
- Varying local safety cultures and practices
- Different regulatory enforcement approaches
- Climate and environmental considerations
- Regional construction methods and materials

**International Experience:**
- Global safety standards and practices
- Cultural considerations in safety programs
- International regulatory frameworks
- Cross-cultural communication skills

# Overcoming Common Experience-Building Challenges

Building practical experience in construction safety isn't always straightforward. Many aspiring professionals face similar challenges that can slow their progress or derail their careers.

### The "Catch-22" Problem
**The Challenge:** Many employers want experienced candidates, but entry-level professionals can't get experience without someone giving them a chance.

**Solutions:**
- Start with internships or volunteer positions
- Consider lateral moves from related fields
- Emphasize transferable skills from other industries
- Network extensively to find champions who will take risks on newcomers
- Consider temporary or contract positions to prove yourself

## Credibility with Experienced Workers

**The Challenge:** Construction workers may be skeptical of safety professionals without hands-on construction experience.

**Solutions:**
- Learn construction processes and terminology
- Spend time understanding each trade's specific challenges
- Ask questions and show genuine interest in their work
- Acknowledge their expertise while sharing safety knowledge
- Build relationships through consistent, respectful interactions

## Geographic Limitations

**The Challenge:** Some areas have limited construction activity or safety opportunities.

**Solutions:**
- Consider relocating to markets with more construction activity
- Look for opportunities in related industries (manufacturing, utilities)
- Explore remote work opportunities with national

- companies
- Build experience through volunteer work and professional organizations
- Network with professionals in other markets

**Financial Pressures**
**The Challenge:** Entry-level safety positions may pay less than other career options, creating financial pressure.

**Solutions:**
- Develop a long-term financial plan that accounts for career growth
- Consider part-time safety work while maintaining other income
- Look for employers who offer tuition assistance or certification support
- Negotiate for professional development opportunities in lieu of higher starting salary
- Remember that safety careers typically offer strong long-term earning potential

# Action Steps for Chapter 8

1. **Identify three entry-level positions that match your current qualifications**
2. **Research internship opportunities at companies in your target market**
3. **Connect with three potential mentors through professional networks**
4. **Volunteer for one professional organization or community safety program**
5. **Create a plan to gain experience in at least two different types of construction**
6. **Network with construction workers to understand their perspectives on safety**
7. **Document your experience-building activities to track progress and create compelling resume**

**content**

## Key Takeaways
- Practical experience is essential for credibility and effectiveness in construction safety
- Multiple pathways exist for gaining experience, from entry-level positions to internships and volunteer work
- Mentorship relationships can dramatically accelerate your professional development
- Diverse experience across project types, company sizes, and geographic markets enhances career prospects
- Common challenges in building experience can be overcome with strategic planning and persistence
- The investment in gaining diverse experience pays dividends throughout your career

Remember Mike Thompson from the beginning of this chapter? His willingness to learn from that experienced electrician led to a mentoring relationship that shaped his entire career. Mike made it a point to work on different types of projects, with various contractors, and in multiple geographic markets. That diverse experience base made him incredibly valuable to employers and ultimately led to his current role overseeing safety for a major national contractor.

Your experience-building journey will be unique to your circumstances and goals, but the principles remain the same: seek diverse experiences, learn from everyone you meet, stay humble and curious, and always remember that every day in the field is an opportunity to learn something that could save someone's life tomorrow. The construction industry respects those who have "been there and done that" - make sure you're building those credentials every step of the way.

# CHAPTER 9: ESSENTIAL SKILLS FOR SAFETY PROFESSIONALS

*"The best safety professionals aren't just rule enforcers - they're problem solvers, communicators, and leaders who can influence change without formal authority."*

As a construction safety professional, your technical knowledge of regulations and hazards is just the foundation. To truly excel in this field, you need to develop a diverse skill set that goes far beyond knowing OSHA standards. This chapter explores the four critical skill areas that separate good safety professionals from great ones: investigation and root cause analysis, training design and delivery, data analysis and reporting, and leadership without authority.

## Investigation and Root Cause Analysis

When incidents occur on construction sites, the immediate response often focuses on treating injuries and securing the scene. However, your role as a safety professional extends much deeper - you must become a detective, uncovering not just what happened, but why it happened and how to prevent it from happening again.

## The Art of Asking Why

Effective incident investigation begins with understanding that most accidents don't have a single cause. Instead, they result from a chain of events, decisions, and conditions that align in the worst possible way. Your job is to identify every link in that chain.

The "Five Whys" technique, developed by Toyota, provides a simple but powerful framework for getting to root causes. When a worker falls from a ladder, asking "why" just once might reveal they weren't using fall protection. But keep asking:

- Why weren't they using fall protection? The harness was in the truck.
- Why was the harness in the truck? They forgot to bring it to the work area.
- Why did they forget? There's no system for tracking PPE distribution.
- Why is there no system? Management hasn't prioritized PPE accountability.
- Why hasn't management prioritized this? They don't understand the true cost of incidents.

Each "why" takes you deeper into the organizational and systemic issues that created the conditions for the accident.

## Gathering Evidence Like a Professional

Your investigation skills must be methodical and thorough. This means arriving at incident scenes with the right mindset and tools. Always carry a camera, measuring tape, notebook, and personal protective equipment. Document everything before anyone moves or cleans anything.

Take photographs from multiple angles, showing both the immediate area and the broader context. Measure distances, heights, and angles. Sketch the scene, even if you're not an artist - your rough drawing might capture spatial relationships that photos miss.

Interview witnesses separately and as soon as possible after the incident. People's memories fade quickly, and they may unconsciously coordinate their stories if they talk to each other first. Ask open-ended questions: "Tell me what you saw" rather than "Did the worker seem rushed?" The first question lets witnesses describe what they observed; the second plants ideas in their minds.

**Root Cause Analysis Methodologies**
While the Five Whys works well for simple incidents, complex accidents require more sophisticated analysis tools. The Management Oversight and Risk Tree (MORT) technique provides a comprehensive framework for examining both the immediate causes and the management system failures that allowed those causes to exist.

Fault Tree Analysis works backward from the incident, mapping out all the possible combinations of events that could have led to the outcome. This visual approach helps you identify multiple contributing factors and understand how they interacted.

The Swiss Cheese Model, developed by James Reason, illustrates how accidents occur when holes in multiple layers of defense align. In construction, these layers might include engineering controls, administrative procedures, training programs, and personal protective equipment. Your investigation should examine each layer to understand where the holes existed and why.

## Developing Corrective Actions That Actually Work

The most thorough investigation is worthless if it doesn't lead to effective corrective actions. Many safety professionals fall into the trap of recommending generic solutions: "Retrain all workers" or "Remind supervisors to enforce rules." These band-aid approaches rarely address the underlying problems.

Effective corrective actions should be specific, measurable, and target the root causes you identified. If your investigation revealed that workers skip safety procedures when they're behind schedule, don't just recommend "better time management training." Instead, examine the project scheduling process, look at productivity incentives, and consider how safety requirements are factored into time estimates.

Always apply the hierarchy of controls when developing recommendations. Engineering controls that eliminate or reduce hazards are more effective than administrative controls that rely on people remembering to follow procedures. If you can't engineer the hazard away, make following procedures as easy as possible and violating them difficult.

# Training Design and Delivery

Construction workers learn differently than office employees. They're often hands-on learners who respond better to demonstration than lengthy lectures. They may have varying levels of formal education and literacy. Some may speak English as a second language or not at all. Understanding these realities is crucial for designing training that actually changes behavior.

## Understanding Your Audience

Before designing any training program, spend time with the workers you'll be teaching. Watch them perform their jobs. Ask about their biggest challenges and frustrations. Understand their work culture and what motivates them.

Construction workers often have a healthy skepticism toward safety training, especially if they've sat through poorly designed programs in the past. They've seen trainers who've never swung a hammer try to tell them how to do their jobs safely. They've endured death-by-PowerPoint sessions that had little relevance to their daily reality.

To overcome this skepticism, you must establish credibility quickly. Share your own construction experience if you have it. If you don't, acknowledge that fact and explain how you've learned about their work. Bring in experienced workers as co-trainers or case study sources. Show that you understand and respect the challenges they face.

## Adult Learning Principles in Action

Adults learn best when they understand why they need to know something and can immediately apply what they've learned. This means starting every training session by explaining not just what you'll cover, but why it matters to their daily work and personal well-being.

Make training interactive from the beginning. Instead of starting with a lecture about fall protection regulations, begin with a scenario: "You're working on a roof when your safety harness gets caught on a piece of equipment. What do you do?" Let participants discuss the situation, then use their responses to introduce the concepts you want to teach.

Use the participants' own experiences as teaching tools. Ask for examples of near-misses or safety challenges they've encountered. These real stories are more powerful than any textbook case study because the learners lived them.

Break up information into digestible chunks. The human brain can only absorb so much at once, especially when learning technical material. Plan frequent breaks and use the time between segments for hands-on activities or discussions.

## Making Safety Training Engaging

Traditional safety training has earned a reputation for being boring, but it doesn't have to be. Construction workers appreciate humor, competition, and practical problem-solving. Use these preferences to your advantage.

Create scenarios that mirror real jobsite conditions. If you're teaching about excavation safety, don't just show pictures of proper shoring techniques - bring in soil samples and let participants feel the difference between stable and unstable earth. Set up mock trenches where they can practice entry procedures.

Use storytelling to make abstract concepts concrete. Instead of reciting statistics about crane accidents, tell the story of a specific incident: what the weather was like that day, what the crew was trying to accomplish, how the sequence of events unfolded. Help learners visualize themselves in similar situations.

Incorporate technology thoughtfully. Virtual reality can provide safe ways to experience dangerous situations. Mobile apps can deliver just-in-time training when workers encounter specific hazards. But remember that technology is a tool, not a solution - it only works if it enhances the learning experience rather than complicating it.

**Measuring Training Effectiveness**
The true test of safety training isn't whether participants can pass a quiz - it's whether they change their behavior on the job. This requires moving beyond traditional training evaluation methods.

Level 1 evaluation (participant reactions) tells you whether people enjoyed the training, but not whether they learned anything useful. Level 2 evaluation (learning assessment) measures knowledge acquisition but doesn't predict behavior change. You need to get to Level 3 (behavior change) and Level 4 (results) to determine real effectiveness.
Follow up with participants weeks or months after training. Observe them at work to see if they're applying what they learned. Ask supervisors whether they've noticed changes in safety behavior. Track incident rates and near-miss reports to identify trends.

Use this feedback to continuously improve your training programs. If participants consistently struggle with certain concepts, find different ways to present that material. If they're not applying specific skills, examine whether there are workplace barriers preventing them from doing so.

# Data Analysis and Reporting

In today's data-driven world, safety professionals must be comfortable collecting, analyzing, and presenting information that tells a compelling story about workplace safety. Raw numbers don't change behavior - meaningful insights do.

## Collecting the Right Data

Not all safety data is created equal. Lagging indicators like injury rates tell you what happened in the past but don't help prevent future incidents. Leading indicators like near-miss reports, safety observation scores, and training completion rates can help you identify problems before they result in injuries.

Develop systems for capturing both types of data consistently. This might mean creating simple reporting forms that workers can complete quickly, setting up digital tools for supervisors to log safety observations, or establishing regular processes for measuring program effectiveness.

Focus on quality over quantity. A few reliable metrics that you track consistently are more valuable than dozens of data points that you collect sporadically. Make sure everyone understands what each metric means and why it matters.

## Turning Numbers into Stories

Construction managers and executives are busy people who need information presented clearly and concisely. They don't want to wade through pages of statistics - they want to understand what the data means for their business and what actions they should take.

Learn to identify trends and patterns in your data. A spike in hand injuries might correlate with the start of a new project using unfamiliar tools. An increase in near-miss reports could indicate improved safety culture rather than declining conditions. Your job is to dig deeper and understand what's really happening.

Create visualizations that make your message clear. A well-designed chart can communicate trends more effectively than paragraphs of text. Use colors and formatting strategically to highlight important information and guide the reader's attention.

## Benchmarking and Context

Safety performance data is most meaningful when compared to relevant benchmarks. Industry averages provide one point of comparison, but they may not reflect your specific circumstances. A high-rise construction company should compare itself to other high-rise builders, not to residential contractors.

Develop internal benchmarks by tracking your own performance over time. This allows you to identify improvements or declining trends specific to your organization. Look for seasonal patterns, project-specific variations, and other factors that might influence your results.

## Communicating Insights Effectively

Your analysis is only valuable if it leads to action. This means presenting findings in ways that resonate with different audiences. Frontline supervisors need practical, actionable information they can use immediately. Senior executives want strategic insights that tie to business objectives.

Tailor your communication style to your audience. Use technical language with safety professionals but plain English with general managers. Include financial implications when presenting to executives - they need to understand how safety performance affects the bottom line.

Tell complete stories with your data. Don't just report what happened - explain why it matters and what should be done about it. Connect safety performance to broader business metrics like productivity, quality, and employee retention.

# Leadership and Influence Without Authority

Perhaps the most challenging aspect of being a construction safety professional is that you're often responsible for outcomes you can't directly control. You need crews to follow safety procedures, but you don't supervise them. You need management to invest in safety improvements, but you don't control the budget. Success requires mastering the art of influence without authority.

## Understanding the Influence Landscape

Construction sites have complex power structures that aren't always reflected in organizational charts. The project superintendent might have formal authority, but the veteran foreman with thirty years of experience often has more influence over how work gets done. Union stewards, lead workers, and informal leaders all play roles in shaping workplace culture.

Map these influence networks early in your role. Identify who the real decision-makers are for different issues. Understand what motivates each key player - some care most about productivity, others about quality, still others about worker welfare. Tailor your approach accordingly.

## Building Credibility and Trust

Your influence depends entirely on your credibility. Construction workers can spot a fake from a mile away, and once you lose their trust, it's nearly impossible to regain it. Credibility comes from demonstrating competence, showing genuine concern for worker welfare, and following through on commitments.

Be visible on the jobsite, but be useful when you're there. Don't just show up to point out violations - come prepared to solve problems. If you notice a safety hazard, help figure out how to address it rather than just writing it up. When workers see you as a resource rather than just an enforcer, they're more likely to seek your input.

Learn the technical aspects of the work being performed. You don't need to be able to operate every piece of equipment, but you should understand the processes well enough to have intelligent conversations about safety challenges. Ask questions that show you're trying to understand, not just find fault.

## Strategies for Influencing Up

Getting management buy-in for safety initiatives requires understanding their priorities and speaking their language. Construction executives care about schedules, budgets, quality, and reputation. Frame your safety proposals in terms of these business drivers.

Instead of asking for money to "improve safety," present proposals that will "reduce project delays caused by incidents" or "protect the company's reputation with key clients." Use data to demonstrate return on investment. Calculate the cost of incidents, including direct costs like medical expenses and workers' compensation, and indirect costs like schedule delays, rework, and damaged reputation.

Propose solutions, not just problems. When you identify safety issues, come prepared with recommendations that consider practical constraints like budgets and schedules. Show that you understand the business challenges and are working to help solve them, not create additional burdens.

## Influencing Across and Down

Peer relationships with project managers, superintendents, and foremen are crucial for safety success. These individuals control the day-to-day decisions that determine whether safety procedures are followed or ignored.

Position yourself as a partner rather than a policeman. Instead of telling a foreman what they're doing wrong, ask how you can help them accomplish their goals safely. Offer to provide additional training, help solve logistical problems, or coordinate with other trades to reduce conflicts.

When working with frontline workers, remember that they face real pressures that can make safety compliance challenging. They may have productivity quotas to meet, uncomfortable protective equipment to wear, or time constraints that make proper procedures seem impossible. Acknowledge these challenges and work together to find practical solutions.

## The Power of Recognition and Relationship

People are more likely to support initiatives when they feel valued and heard. Look for opportunities to recognize good safety performance publicly. When a crew completes a challenging task without incidents, make sure their achievement is acknowledged. When someone suggests a safety improvement, implement it if possible and give them credit.

Build relationships during calm periods so you have social capital to draw on during crises. Take time for informal conversations. Remember personal details about the people you work with. Show genuine interest in their success, not just their safety compliance.

**Dealing with Resistance**
Not everyone will embrace your safety initiatives enthusiastically. Some resistance comes from practical concerns - people may genuinely believe that safety requirements will make their jobs harder or less efficient. Other resistance is cultural or emotional, rooted in skepticism about management intentions or previous bad experiences with safety programs.

Address practical concerns with data and demonstration. If workers believe that safety equipment slows them down, measure actual productivity with and without the equipment. Often, the perceived impact is greater than the real impact. If there is a legitimate productivity cost, work to minimize it through better equipment selection or process improvements.

Cultural resistance requires patience and persistence. Focus on building relationships with informal leaders who can help shift attitudes over time. Share stories that illustrate why safety matters without being preachy. Celebrate small wins to build momentum for bigger changes.

## Developing Your Professional Toolkit
The skills described in this chapter don't develop overnight. They require continuous practice, feedback, and refinement. Create opportunities to exercise these abilities even when you're not facing major incidents or crises.

Volunteer to investigate minor incidents and near-misses to build your analysis skills. Offer to deliver safety talks at team meetings to practice training and presentation abilities. Take on data analysis projects that help you become more comfortable with numbers and trends. Look for chances to influence outcomes through collaboration rather than authority.

Seek feedback from colleagues, supervisors, and the workers you serve. Ask what's working well and what could be improved. Be open to criticism and willing to adjust your approach based on what you learn.

Consider joining professional organizations where you can learn from experienced safety professionals and share your own insights. Attend conferences, participate in webinars, and engage in online forums where safety topics are discussed.

## The Integration Challenge

These four skill areas don't operate in isolation - they reinforce and build upon each other. Your investigation skills inform your training design by revealing the real reasons why incidents occur. Your data analysis capabilities help you measure training effectiveness and identify areas where your influence efforts are succeeding or falling short. Your leadership abilities determine whether your investigation findings and training recommendations are actually implemented.

The most successful safety professionals learn to weave these skills together seamlessly. They use investigation insights to design targeted training programs, analyze data to demonstrate the value of safety investments, and leverage their influence to ensure that corrective actions are implemented and sustained.

## Looking Forward

As you develop these essential skills, remember that they're not just tools for preventing accidents - they're the foundation for building a career that makes a real difference in people's lives. Every thorough investigation that prevents future incidents, every training session that changes behavior, every data analysis that drives better decisions, and every successful influence effort that improves safety culture represents lives saved and families protected.

The construction industry needs safety professionals who can do more than recite regulations. It needs problem solvers, teachers, analysts, and leaders who can navigate complex challenges and drive meaningful change. By mastering these essential skills, you position yourself to be one of those professionals who doesn't just enforce safety rules, but transforms safety culture.

In the next chapter, we'll explore how to apply these skills in developing comprehensive safety programs that address the full range of construction hazards and organizational challenges. The foundation you've built through investigation, training, data analysis, and influence will serve as the cornerstone for creating systematic approaches to construction safety management.

# CHAPTER 10: DEVELOPING EFFECTIVE SAFETY PROGRAMS

*"A safety program isn't a binder full of policies gathering dust on a shelf - it's a living system that guides daily decisions and transforms workplace culture."*

Building an effective safety program is like constructing a building: you need a solid foundation, a clear blueprint, quality materials, and skilled execution. But unlike a building that serves its purpose simply by existing, a safety program only works when it's actively used by real people facing real hazards every day.

This chapter will guide you through the process of developing comprehensive safety programs that don't just meet regulatory requirements, but actually prevent injuries and save lives. We'll explore how to structure programs for maximum effectiveness, set meaningful goals, create practical policies and procedures, and integrate safety seamlessly with project management processes.

## Program Structure and Key Elements
### The Architecture of Safety

Every effective safety program is built on four foundational pillars: leadership commitment, worker involvement, hazard identification and control, and continuous improvement. These aren't just bureaucratic requirements - they're the essential elements that determine whether your program will succeed or fail.

**Leadership Commitment** goes far beyond having executives sign a safety policy. True commitment means leaders actively participate in safety activities, allocate necessary resources, and hold themselves accountable for safety performance. When a project manager delays a concrete pour because weather conditions aren't safe, that's leadership commitment in action. When a company invests in better scaffolding even though the old equipment meets minimum standards, that's commitment.

Look for ways to make leadership commitment visible and concrete. This might mean having executives participate in safety walks, requiring management attendance at incident reviews, or including safety performance in leadership evaluations. The key is ensuring that words align with actions consistently over time.

**Worker Involvement** transforms safety from something that's done to workers into something they actively participate in. Construction workers are on the front lines - they see hazards first, understand job realities best, and know which solutions will actually work. Programs that tap into this knowledge are invariably more effective than those developed in isolation.

Create multiple channels for worker input. Safety committees provide formal venues for ongoing dialogue. Suggestion systems allow anonymous feedback. Regular safety meetings enable real-time problem-solving. Job hazard analyses engage workers in identifying and controlling risks before work begins.

**Hazard Identification and Control** is the technical heart of your program. This element encompasses everything from initial hazard assessments to ongoing monitoring and control. It includes both proactive identification of potential problems and reactive investigation of incidents that do occur.

The most effective programs use multiple methods for hazard identification: formal inspections, worker reports, near-miss investigations, job hazard analyses, and pre-task planning. They also apply the hierarchy of controls systematically, prioritizing elimination and engineering controls over administrative measures and personal protective equipment.

**Continuous Improvement** ensures your program evolves with changing conditions, new hazards, and lessons learned. Construction is a dynamic industry - new technologies, materials, and methods constantly emerge. Regulations change. Worker demographics shift. Programs that don't adapt become obsolete.

Build improvement mechanisms into your program structure. Regular program reviews should examine both performance data and stakeholder feedback. Incident investigations should generate specific recommendations for program updates. Industry best practices should be evaluated and incorporated when appropriate.

## The Program Hierarchy

Effective safety programs operate at multiple levels, each

serving specific purposes and audiences. Understanding this hierarchy helps ensure your program components work together rather than creating confusion or conflict.

**Program-level documents** establish the overall framework and philosophy. This includes your safety policy, program manual, and organizational procedures. These documents should be relatively stable - they shouldn't change frequently, but they should be comprehensive enough to guide decision-making across diverse situations.

**Project-level documents** adapt the overall program to specific job conditions. Site-specific safety plans, activity hazard analyses, and project safety rules fall into this category. These documents should be developed collaboratively with project teams and updated as conditions change.

**Task-level documents** provide specific guidance for individual activities. Job safety analyses, safe work procedures, and pre-task briefing forms belong here. These should be practical tools that workers can use in real-time to make safe decisions.

**Personal-level tools** help individual workers manage their own safety. Training records, competency assessments, and personal protective equipment assignments fit this category. These tools should be easily accessible and regularly updated.

## Setting Measurable Goals and Objectives
### Beyond Zero Injuries

Most construction companies claim their safety goal is "zero injuries," but this aspiration, while admirable, doesn't provide useful guidance for day-to-day decision-making. Effective safety programs need specific, measurable objectives that drive behavior and enable progress tracking.

Start by understanding your current performance baseline.

Analyze at least three years of injury data to identify patterns. Look beyond simple frequency rates - examine severity, body parts affected, causes, and demographics. This analysis reveals where your biggest opportunities lie.

Consider both lagging and leading indicators when setting goals. Lagging indicators like injury rates tell you what happened in the past. Leading indicators like training completion rates, safety observation scores, and near-miss reporting levels help predict future performance.

**Lagging Indicator Goals** might include:
- Reduce recordable injury rate by 20% compared to previous year
- Achieve total recordable incident rate below industry average
- Eliminate fatalities and life-threatening injuries
- Reduce workers' compensation costs by 15%

**Leading Indicator Goals** might include:
- Complete 100% of planned safety training within 30 days of hire
- Conduct safety observations on 25% of active work areas weekly
- Investigate 100% of near-miss reports within 24 hours
- Achieve 95% compliance scores on safety audits

**SMART Goal Framework**
Apply the SMART criteria (Specific, Measurable, Achievable, Relevant, Time-bound) to ensure your safety objectives drive real improvement rather than just looking good on paper.

**Specific** goals clearly define what success looks like. Instead of "improve fall protection compliance," try "ensure 100% of workers at heights above 6 feet use appropriate fall protection systems as verified by weekly safety observations."

**Measurable** goals include quantifiable targets that can be tracked objectively. This might be percentages, rates, counts, or other numerical measures. The key is having clear criteria for success that don't depend on subjective judgment.

**Achievable** goals stretch performance without being impossible. Goals that are too easy don't drive improvement. Goals that are impossible discourage effort. The sweet spot challenges people to perform better while remaining within the realm of possibility.

**Relevant** goals address your most significant safety challenges and align with business objectives. A goal to reduce hand injuries makes sense if hand injuries are a major problem for your organization. If your primary challenge is falls, focus there first.

**Time-bound** goals include specific deadlines that create urgency and enable progress tracking. Annual goals provide overall direction, but consider quarterly or monthly milestones that maintain momentum and allow for course corrections.

### Cascading Goals Through the Organization

Safety goals should cascade from the corporate level down to individual projects and workers. This alignment ensures everyone is working toward the same objectives while allowing for local adaptation.

Corporate goals typically focus on overall performance metrics and strategic initiatives. Division or regional goals might address specific operational challenges or market conditions. Project goals should reflect local hazards and conditions while supporting higher-level objectives.

Individual goals might include personal development objectives like completing specific training or achieving safety leadership roles. Supervisor goals could include team performance metrics and program implementation responsibilities.

## Creating Policies and Procedures
### The Policy Foundation
Safety policies establish the fundamental principles that guide all safety-related decisions in your organization.
They should be clear, comprehensive, and aligned with your company's values and business objectives.
An effective safety policy typically includes:
- A statement of management commitment to safety
- The organization's safety philosophy and core values
- General responsibilities for different organizational levels
- Authority and accountability structures
- Resource allocation commitments
- Performance expectations and consequences

Keep policy language clear and action-oriented. Avoid legal jargon that obscures meaning. Instead of "The organization shall endeavor to minimize exposure to potentially hazardous conditions," try "We will identify and control hazards before they can cause injuries."

Make sure policies are realistic and achievable. Policies that require perfect compliance with impossible standards actually undermine safety by encouraging workarounds and creating cynicism. If you can't enforce a policy consistently, don't create it.

### Developing Practical Procedures

While policies establish principles, procedures provide step-by-step guidance for implementing those principles in specific situations. Effective procedures bridge the gap between high-level commitments and daily work activities.

**Procedure Development Process:**
1. **Identify the need** - What specific safety challenge does this procedure address? Is it required by regulation? Driven by incident experience? Requested by field personnel?
2. **Gather input** - Who needs to be involved in developing this procedure? Include subject matter experts, affected workers, supervisors, and anyone else who will use or implement the procedure.
3. **Research best practices** - What do regulations require? What do industry standards recommend? How do other successful organizations handle similar challenges?
4. **Draft the procedure** - Write clear, sequential steps that can be followed by someone with appropriate training and experience. Use active voice and specific language.
5. **Test and refine** - Pilot the procedure with a small group before full implementation. Gather feedback and make necessary adjustments.
6. **Implement and train** - Roll out the procedure with appropriate training and support. Ensure everyone who needs to use it understands both the steps and the reasons behind them.
7. **Monitor and improve** - Track compliance and effectiveness. Gather ongoing feedback and update the procedure as needed.

## Making Procedures User-Friendly

Construction workers often view safety procedures as obstacles to getting work done efficiently. This perception usually stems from procedures that are poorly written, impractical, or disconnected from job realities.

## Design for the Real World

Visit job sites and observe the work your procedures are supposed to govern. Talk to workers about challenges they face. Understand the time pressures, space constraints, and resource limitations that affect how work gets done.

Build flexibility into procedures where possible. Instead of specifying exactly which brand of safety equipment to use, establish performance criteria that allow for different options. This accommodates varying job conditions while maintaining safety standards.

Consider environmental factors that affect procedure implementation. A procedure that works well in good weather might be impractical during rain or high winds. Include guidance for different conditions or specify when work should be suspended.

## Use Clear, Action-Oriented Language

Write procedures in the active voice using simple, direct language. Instead of "Fall protection shall be utilized by personnel," write "Workers must wear fall protection harnesses."

Use parallel structure for sequential steps. Start each step with an action verb: "Inspect the harness," "Attach the lanyard," "Test the connection." This makes procedures easier to follow and remember.

Include the "why" behind critical steps. When workers understand the reasons for requirements, they're more likely to comply consistently. "Test the connection by pulling firmly on the lanyard to ensure it won't detach under load."

**Visual Aids and Job Aids**
Supplement written procedures with visual aids that clarify complex steps or show proper equipment setup. Photos, diagrams, and flowcharts can communicate information more effectively than text alone.

Create job aids that workers can reference in the field. Laminated cards, mobile apps, or simple checklists help ensure procedures are followed correctly even when workers are under pressure.

Consider language barriers and literacy levels when designing procedures. Use more visuals and simpler language for diverse workforces. Translate critical procedures into languages spoken by significant portions of your workforce.

# Integration with Project Management
## Safety as a Project Function
The most effective construction safety programs integrate seamlessly with project management processes rather than operating as separate, parallel systems. This integration ensures that safety considerations influence project decisions from the earliest planning stages through final completion.

**Pre-Construction Integration**
Safety planning should begin during the estimating and bidding process. Identify major safety challenges and include appropriate time and resources in project schedules and budgets. This might include specialized equipment, additional

training, or extended durations for high-risk activities.

Develop site-specific safety plans as part of overall project planning. These plans should address known hazards, establish safety protocols, identify resource requirements, and define communication procedures. They should be working documents that guide daily decisions, not just compliance paperwork.

Include safety considerations in subcontractor selection and management. Evaluate potential subcontractors' safety performance, require appropriate insurance coverage, and establish clear safety expectations in contract documents.

**Daily Operation Integration**
Make safety planning part of routine project activities. Morning planning meetings should include safety considerations alongside schedule and resource discussions.

Weekly look-ahead planning should identify upcoming safety challenges and ensure appropriate preparations.
Integrate safety observations into quality control processes. Supervisors conducting quality inspections can simultaneously observe safety compliance and conditions. This dual focus reinforces the connection between safety and quality performance.

Include safety performance in project reporting and communication. Regular project reports should include safety metrics alongside schedule and cost information. This visibility ensures safety receives appropriate management attention.

**Resource Allocation and Scheduling**
Build safety requirements into project schedules rather than treating them as add-ons that can be compressed when time gets tight. If a task requires specific safety equipment or setup

time, include that in the schedule.

Consider safety implications when making trade-offs between time, cost, and quality. Understand that shortcuts that compromise safety often create hidden costs through incidents, rework, and reputation damage.

Plan for weather and seasonal variations that affect safety requirements. Hot weather might require additional breaks and hydration measures. Cold weather could necessitate different protective equipment or modified procedures.

## Technology Integration

Modern construction projects increasingly rely on technology for project management, and safety programs should leverage these same tools and systems.

### Digital Documentation

Use project management software to track safety deliverables alongside other project requirements. This might include training completions, inspection schedules, or corrective action items. Integration ensures safety tasks don't fall through the cracks.

Implement mobile tools that allow field personnel to report safety observations, near-misses, and incidents in real-time. Photos, GPS coordinates, and immediate notifications can significantly improve response times and documentation quality.

Consider wearable technology that can monitor worker location, movement, and environmental conditions. While these tools raise privacy concerns that must be addressed, they can provide valuable data for improving safety performance.

## Data Integration and Analysis

Connect safety data with other project metrics to identify correlations and trends. You might discover that safety incidents increase when projects fall behind schedule, or that certain types of work consistently generate more safety challenges.

Use business intelligence tools to create dashboards that provide real-time visibility into safety performance. Project managers can see safety metrics alongside schedule and cost data, enabling integrated decision-making.

Develop predictive analytics that identify projects or activities at higher risk for safety incidents. This early warning capability allows for proactive intervention before problems occur.

# Program Implementation Strategy
## Phased Rollout Approach

Implementing a comprehensive safety program all at once can overwhelm organizations and lead to incomplete adoption. A phased approach allows for learning, adjustment, and building momentum over time.

### Phase 1: Foundation Building
- Establish leadership commitment and accountability
- Develop core policies and procedures
- Implement basic hazard identification and control measures
- Begin data collection and analysis systems

### Phase 2: System Development
- Expand training programs and worker involvement
- Enhance incident investigation and corrective action processes

- Implement leading indicator measurement systems
- Strengthen contractor safety requirements

**Phase 3: Advanced Implementation**
- Deploy technology solutions and data analytics
- Develop behavior-based safety initiatives
- Implement advanced risk management techniques
- Establish benchmarking and continuous improvement processes

## Change Management Considerations

Safety program implementation is fundamentally a change management challenge. People must adopt new behaviors, processes, and ways of thinking. Understanding and addressing resistance is crucial for success.

**Common Sources of Resistance:**
- Fear that safety requirements will slow down work
- Skepticism about management commitment
- Previous negative experiences with safety programs
- Lack of understanding about why changes are necessary
- Concerns about increased scrutiny or discipline

**Strategies for Overcoming Resistance:**
- Communicate the business case for safety clearly and repeatedly
- Involve skeptics in program development and implementation
- Demonstrate quick wins that show program value
- Address practical concerns about implementation challenges
- Recognize and reward early adopters and champions

## Success Metrics and Milestones

Define clear metrics for measuring program implementation success. These should include both process measures (what you're doing) and outcome measures (what you're achieving).

**Process Measures:**
- Percentage of workers trained on new procedures
- Number of safety observations completed
- Compliance rates for key safety requirements
- Participation levels in safety committees and meetings

**Outcome Measures:**
- Injury and incident rates
- Near-miss reporting levels
- Safety audit scores
- Worker engagement survey results

Establish milestone reviews at regular intervals to assess progress and make necessary adjustments. These reviews should examine both quantitative data and qualitative feedback from stakeholders.

## Sustaining Program Effectiveness
### Avoiding Program Decay
Even well-designed safety programs can lose effectiveness over time if they're not actively maintained and continuously improved. Program decay often occurs gradually, making it difficult to detect until significant deterioration has occurred.

**Warning Signs of Program Decay:**
- Declining participation in safety activities
- Increasing compliance violations
- Lengthening response times for corrective actions
- Reduced management engagement
- Growing cynicism about safety initiatives

**Prevention Strategies:**
- Regular program audits and assessments
- Continuous stakeholder feedback collection
- Ongoing training and refresher programs
- Leadership engagement and accountability

- Recognition and celebration of achievements

**Continuous Improvement Culture**

Transform your safety program from a compliance exercise into a learning system that continuously evolves and improves. This requires creating a culture where experimentation, feedback, and adaptation are valued and rewarded.

Encourage innovation and creative problem-solving in safety management. When workers identify better ways to accomplish tasks safely, test their ideas and implement successful innovations. This approach harnesses the collective intelligence of your workforce.

Learn from both successes and failures. When safety initiatives work well, understand why and apply those lessons elsewhere. When programs fall short, analyze the reasons and use that knowledge to improve future efforts.

Stay connected with industry developments and best practices. Participate in safety conferences, join professional organizations, and maintain networks with other safety professionals. The construction industry is constantly evolving, and your safety program should evolve with it.

# Looking Ahead

Developing an effective safety program is not a destination - it's an ongoing journey of improvement and adaptation. The foundation you build today will support your organization's safety efforts for years to come, but it must be continuously strengthened and updated to remain effective.

Remember that the ultimate test of your safety program isn't whether it looks good on paper or satisfies auditors - it's whether it prevents injuries and saves lives. Every policy, procedure, and process should be evaluated against this fundamental criterion.

In the next chapter, we'll explore how to bring your safety program to life through effective training and communication. The strongest program framework is worthless if people don't understand it, believe in it, and apply it consistently in their daily work. We'll examine how to design and deliver training that changes behavior and communication strategies that build genuine safety culture.

Your safety program is the foundation upon which all other safety efforts are built. Take the time to build it right, and it will serve as a powerful tool for protecting the people who depend on your expertise and leadership.

# CHAPTER 11: TRAINING AND COMMUNICATION

Safety training isn't just about checking boxes or meeting regulatory requirements - it's about creating genuine understanding that keeps workers alive and healthy. As a construction safety professional, your ability to effectively train and communicate will directly impact lives. This chapter will equip you with the knowledge and skills to design, deliver, and evaluate safety training that actually changes behavior and reduces incidents.

## The Foundation: Adult Learning Principles

Before diving into specific training methods, you must understand how adults learn differently from children. Adult learning theory, developed by Malcolm Knowles, provides the framework for effective safety training.

### Key Principles of Adult Learning
**Adults are self-directed learners.** They want to know why

they need to learn something before they invest time and energy in learning it. Don't just tell a roofer to wear a harness - explain how fall protection has saved lives and prevented permanent disabilities. Share statistics about fall injuries in construction and let them connect the dots.

**Adults bring experience to the learning process.** Your trainees aren't blank slates. They've been working, sometimes for decades, and have developed their own approaches to getting the job done. Respect this experience while helping them see new perspectives. Ask questions like, "What have you seen happen when someone took a shortcut?" or "Tell me about a time you saw someone do something unsafe."

**Adults learn best when the material is immediately applicable.** Abstract concepts don't stick unless workers can see how they apply to their daily tasks. When teaching about respiratory protection, don't just explain the types of respirators - show them the specific respirator they'll use on their current project and practice putting it on correctly.

**Adults are problem-centered, not subject-centered.** Frame your training around solving real problems they face on the job. Instead of a general presentation on "Electrical Safety," focus on "How to Safely Work Around Overhead Power Lines on Your Current Project."

## Applying Adult Learning Principles to Safety Training

Start every training session by explaining the "what's in it for me" factor. Workers need to understand not just what they should do, but why it matters to them personally. Connect safety practices to their ability to go home healthy to their families, maintain their earning capacity, and take pride in their professional skills.

Use their experiences as teaching tools. When someone shares a story about a near-miss or incident, explore what happened and what could have been done differently. This approach makes the learning more memorable and relevant than any PowerPoint presentation.

Build in opportunities for practice and feedback. Safety isn't learned through lectures alone - it requires hands-on practice. Whether it's properly setting up fall protection, using a multimeter to test for electrical hazards, or conducting a pre-use inspection of equipment, workers need to practice these skills until they become automatic.

## Designing Effective Toolbox Talks

Toolbox talks are the backbone of ongoing safety communication in construction. These brief, focused discussions happen regularly - often daily - and address specific hazards or safety topics relevant to the current work. Done well, they're powerful tools for reinforcing safety culture. Done poorly, they become meaningless rituals that workers tune out.

### Elements of Effective Toolbox Talks

**Keep them short and focused.** Fifteen minutes is typically the maximum attention span you'll get from workers who are eager to start their day. Pick one topic and cover it thoroughly rather than trying to address multiple issues superficially.

**Make them interactive.** The most effective toolbox talks involve workers in the discussion. Ask questions, encourage sharing of experiences, and get people talking. Questions like "What hazards might we encounter today?" or "Who has seen this type of incident before?" get people engaged and thinking.

**Connect to the day's work.** Generic talks about safety in general are less effective than specific discussions about the hazards workers will face that day. If the crew is working on scaffolding, talk about scaffold safety. If they're working in a confined space, focus on atmospheric testing and emergency procedures.

**Use visual aids and props.** Bring the actual equipment you're discussing. Show the difference between a damaged and proper sling. Demonstrate the correct way to set up a ladder. Let workers handle the equipment and ask questions.

**Document the discussion.** Keep records of who attended, what was covered, and any questions or concerns raised. This documentation serves multiple purposes: it shows due diligence in training, helps you track which topics you've covered, and provides a record of worker engagement with safety topics.

**Common Toolbox Talk Mistakes to Avoid**
Don't read from a script or PowerPoint slides. Workers can sense when you're just going through the motions, and they'll respond in kind. Know your material well enough to speak conversationally about it.

Avoid covering too many topics in one session. It's better to thoroughly discuss one hazard than to superficially mention five. Workers are more likely to remember and apply information when it's focused and detailed.

Don't ignore questions or concerns. If a worker raises an issue, address it directly or commit to finding the answer. Dismissing questions undermines your credibility and discourages future participation.

# Conducting Effective Safety Meetings

While toolbox talks are brief and focused, safety meetings provide opportunities for more comprehensive training and discussion. These longer sessions allow you to cover complex topics, conduct hands-on training, and address broader safety culture issues.

## Planning Your Safety Meeting

**Set clear objectives.** What do you want workers to know, understand, or be able to do by the end of the meeting? Write these objectives down and refer to them as you plan your content and activities.

**Know your audience.** Consider the experience level, primary language, and specific job responsibilities of your attendees. A meeting for new hires will be very different from one for experienced supervisors.

**Prepare your materials in advance.** Gather any equipment, handouts, or visual aids you'll need. Test any technology you plan to use. Have a backup plan in case equipment fails.

**Choose an appropriate location.** The meeting space should be comfortable, well-lit, and free from distractions. If you're demonstrating equipment or procedures, ensure you have adequate space for hands-on activities.

## Meeting Structure and Flow

**Open with purpose and expectations.** Start by explaining what you'll cover and why it's important to them. Set ground rules for participation and let people know how long the meeting will last.

**Use the "tell, show, do" method.** First, explain the

concept or procedure. Then, demonstrate it yourself. Finally, have participants practice while you provide guidance and feedback.

**Encourage questions and discussion.** Create a safe environment where workers feel comfortable asking questions, sharing concerns, or admitting they don't understand something. Some of the most valuable learning happens during these unscripted moments.

**Summarize key points.** End with a clear summary of the main takeaways. What are the three most important things you want them to remember? What specific actions should they take based on what they've learned?

**Evaluate understanding.** Use questions, scenarios, or brief demonstrations to check that workers understand the material. Don't assume that because you presented information clearly, everyone absorbed it correctly.

# Multilingual and Multicultural Considerations

Construction workforces are increasingly diverse, with workers speaking various languages and coming from different cultural backgrounds. Effective safety professionals must adapt their communication and training approaches to reach all workers effectively.

### Language Barriers and Solutions

**Assess language needs.** Determine what languages are spoken by your workforce and the English proficiency levels of non-native speakers. Don't assume that workers who speak some English understand complex safety concepts in English.

**Provide materials in multiple languages.** Key safety information, including written procedures, signs, and training materials, should be available in the primary languages of your workforce. However, translation isn't enough - materials must be culturally appropriate and written at an appropriate literacy level.

**Use qualified interpreters.** When conducting training for non-English speakers, use professional interpreters who understand construction terminology and safety concepts. Family members or other workers may not accurately convey technical information.

**Employ visual communication.** Pictures, diagrams, and demonstrations can transcend language barriers. Use visual aids to supplement verbal communication, but remember that even images can be interpreted differently across cultures.

**Speak clearly and simply.** When working with non-native English speakers, speak slowly, use simple sentence structures, and avoid idioms or slang. Check for understanding frequently by asking questions or requesting demonstrations.

## Cultural Considerations in Safety Training

**Understand cultural attitudes toward authority.** In some cultures, questioning authority or admitting lack of understanding is considered disrespectful. Workers from these backgrounds may not ask questions even when they don't understand something. Create alternative ways for them to seek clarification privately.

**Recognize different communication styles.** Some cultures

value direct communication, while others prefer indirect approaches. Pay attention to non-verbal cues and be prepared to adapt your communication style to be more effective with different groups.

**Address family and economic pressures.** Workers may feel pressure to work unsafely due to economic needs or family obligations. Acknowledge these pressures while emphasizing that long-term earning capacity depends on staying healthy and avoiding injuries.

**Respect religious and cultural practices.** Be aware of religious holidays, prayer times, and cultural practices that may affect training scheduling or safety practices. For example, some religious head coverings may require special consideration when selecting hard hats or respirators.

# Using Technology for Training Delivery

Technology offers new opportunities to enhance safety training effectiveness, but it should supplement, not replace, human interaction and hands-on practice.

## Digital Training Platforms

**Learning Management Systems (LMS).** These platforms allow you to deliver consistent training content, track completion rates, and maintain training records. They're particularly useful for organizations with multiple locations or large numbers of workers.

**Mobile Learning Apps.** Workers can access safety information, take refresher courses, or report hazards using smartphone apps. This approach is especially effective for just-in-time training when workers encounter unfamiliar situations.

**Online Modules and Courses.** While not suitable for all safety topics, online training can be effective for knowledge-based content like regulations, hazard recognition, and safety procedures. However, hands-on skills still require in-person practice.

### Virtual and Augmented Reality
**Immersive Training Experiences.** VR can provide realistic training scenarios without exposing workers to actual hazards. Workers can practice responding to emergencies, working at height, or operating equipment in a controlled environment.

**Augmented Reality Applications.** AR can overlay safety information onto real-world environments, providing guidance and warnings as workers perform tasks. This technology is still emerging but shows promise for just-in-time training and hazard identification.

### Video and Multimedia
**Training Videos.** Well-produced videos can demonstrate proper procedures, show the consequences of unsafe practices, and provide consistent messaging. However, videos should be supplemented with discussion and hands-on practice.

**Case Study Documentation.** Use photos and videos to document incidents, near-misses, and exemplary safety practices. These real-world examples are often more impactful than generic training materials.

### Technology Implementation Best Practices
**Start with learning objectives.** Choose technology that supports your training goals, not technology for its own sake. The most sophisticated platform is useless if it doesn't help

workers learn what they need to know.

**Ensure accessibility.** Not all workers are comfortable with technology, and some may have limited access to devices or internet connectivity. Provide alternatives and support for those who need it.

**Maintain the human element.** Technology should enhance, not replace, human interaction in safety training. Workers still need opportunities to ask questions, practice skills, and receive feedback from experienced professionals.

**Keep content current.** Digital content can become outdated quickly. Establish processes for regularly reviewing and updating technology-based training materials.

# Measuring Training Effectiveness

Training isn't successful simply because it was delivered - it's successful when it changes behavior and reduces incidents. Measuring training effectiveness helps you improve your programs and demonstrate their value to management.

### Kirkpatrick's Four Levels of Evaluation

**Level 1: Reaction.** Did participants enjoy the training and find it relevant? While positive reactions don't guarantee learning, negative reactions can indicate problems with content or delivery.

**Level 2: Learning.** Did participants acquire the intended knowledge, skills, and attitudes? This can be measured through tests, demonstrations, or observations.

**Level 3: Behavior.** Are participants applying what they learned on the job? This requires observation over time and may involve supervisors or safety professionals monitoring work practices.

**Level 4: Results.** Has the training contributed to improved safety outcomes? This is measured through incident rates, near-miss reports, safety audit scores, and other organizational metrics.

## Practical Evaluation Methods

**Pre- and Post-Training Assessments.** Test knowledge before and after training to measure learning gains. Keep assessments focused on key concepts and avoid making them punitive.

**Behavioral Observations.** Observe workers on the job to see if they're applying safe work practices. Document both positive behaviors and areas for improvement.

**Follow-Up Surveys.** Several weeks after training, survey participants about what they remember, what they've applied, and what barriers they've encountered.

**Incident and Near-Miss Analysis.** Track whether training topics correlate with reductions in related incidents. If you provide ladder safety training, do ladder-related incidents decrease?

## Using Evaluation Results for Improvement

**Identify Knowledge Gaps.** If post-training assessments reveal that workers aren't grasping certain concepts, revise your training approach or spend more time on those topics.

**Address Implementation Barriers.** If workers understand the training but aren't applying it, investigate what's preventing them from using safe practices. Common barriers include time pressure, lack of equipment, or conflicting instructions from supervisors.

**Refine Training Methods.** If certain training techniques consistently produce better results, incorporate them into more of your programs. If some methods aren't working, replace them with more effective approaches.

**Demonstrate Value.** Use evaluation results to show management how training contributes to safety performance and business outcomes. This data supports requests for training resources and reinforces the importance of safety in organizational culture.

# Building a Culture of Continuous Learning

Effective safety training isn't a one-time event - it's an ongoing process that becomes embedded in the organization's culture. Your role is to create an environment where learning about safety is valued, expected, and supported.

## Encouraging Worker Participation

**Make it relevant.** Connect training to workers' immediate needs and concerns. When workers see direct benefits from safety training, they're more likely to engage actively.

**Recognize expertise.** Experienced workers have valuable knowledge to share. Create opportunities for them to teach others and contribute to training programs.

**Provide incentives.** While safety should be valued for its own sake, recognition and rewards can encourage participation in voluntary training programs.

**Remove barriers.** Schedule training at convenient times,

provide necessary resources, and ensure that workers won't be penalized for taking time to learn.

## Creating Learning Opportunities
**Mentorship Programs.** Pair experienced workers with newcomers to provide ongoing guidance and support. This creates opportunities for informal learning and helps maintain safety culture.

**Peer Learning Groups.** Encourage workers to share experiences, discuss challenges, and learn from each other. These groups can be particularly effective for addressing specific trades or specialized tasks.

**Lessons Learned Sessions.** After incidents, near-misses, or successful projects, conduct sessions to discuss what was learned and how practices can be improved.

**Cross-Training Opportunities.** When workers understand different aspects of the construction process, they're better able to identify hazards that might affect their coworkers.

Training and communication are among the most critical skills you'll develop as a construction safety professional. Your ability to effectively share knowledge, change attitudes, and influence behavior will determine your success in protecting workers' lives and health. Remember that every training session is an opportunity to prevent an injury, save a life, or help someone go home safely to their family.

The principles and techniques outlined in this chapter provide a foundation for effective safety training, but they must be adapted to your specific workplace, workforce, and circumstances. Continuously seek feedback, evaluate your effectiveness, and refine your approaches.

The investment you make in developing your training and communication skills will pay dividends throughout your career and in the lives of the workers you serve.

In the next chapter, we'll explore how to investigate incidents and analyze their root causes - skills that complement your training abilities and help you understand what additional training or system improvements may be needed to prevent future incidents.

# CHAPTER 12: INCIDENT INVESTIGATION AND ANALYSIS

When an incident occurs on a construction site, the immediate response focuses on providing aid to injured workers and securing the scene. But once the emergency passes, the real work begins: understanding what happened, why it happened, and how to prevent it from happening again. This chapter will equip you with the knowledge and skills to conduct thorough, effective incident investigations that lead to meaningful improvements in workplace safety.

Incident investigation is both an art and a science. It requires technical knowledge, analytical skills, and the ability to work with people who may be stressed, defensive, or reluctant to share information. Done correctly, investigations become powerful tools for learning and prevention. Done poorly, they become exercises in blame assignment that make future incidents more likely.

# The Purpose and Goals of Incident Investigation

Before diving into investigation techniques, it's crucial to understand what you're trying to achieve. The primary purpose of incident investigation is not to assign blame or determine fault - it's to identify the underlying causes that contributed to the incident so they can be addressed to prevent recurrence.

## Learning, Not Blaming

The most important principle of effective incident investigation is focusing on systems and processes rather than individual actions. While people make mistakes, those mistakes usually occur within systems that allowed or even encouraged unsafe behavior. Your goal is to understand the chain of events and decisions that led to the incident, not to find someone to punish.

This approach requires a fundamental shift in thinking for many organizations. Traditional accident investigations often focus on finding the "root cause" - usually identified as human error - and stopping there. Modern investigation techniques recognize that human error is rarely the true root cause. Instead, it's a symptom of deeper organizational, systemic, or design issues.

## Prevention Through Understanding

Every incident provides valuable information about weaknesses in your safety management system. A near-miss today could be a fatality tomorrow if the underlying causes aren't addressed. By thoroughly investigating all incidents - not just those resulting in serious injuries - you can identify patterns, trends, and systemic issues that need attention.

Consider incidents as "free lessons" that reveal problems in your safety systems. The goal is to learn as much as possible from each event to prevent similar occurrences.

This learning extends beyond the specific hazards involved in the incident to broader questions about training, supervision, communication, and organizational culture.

### Legal and Regulatory Compliance
While learning and prevention are the primary goals, incident investigations also serve important legal and regulatory functions. OSHA requires employers to investigate workplace incidents and maintain records of their findings. Insurance companies expect thorough investigations to support claims processing and risk management. In some cases, investigation findings may be needed for legal proceedings.

However, these compliance requirements should not drive the investigation process. Focus on understanding and prevention, and the compliance requirements will naturally be satisfied. If you start with the goal of protecting the organization legally, you're likely to miss important learning opportunities and may even make the situation worse.

## Investigation Methodologies
Several proven methodologies exist for conducting incident investigations. Each has its strengths and is suited to different types of incidents and organizational contexts. Understanding these approaches will help you choose the right tool for each situation.

### The 5 Whys Technique
The 5 Whys is a simple but powerful questioning technique that helps you dig beneath surface causes to

identify underlying issues. The process involves asking "why" repeatedly until you reach the root causes of the incident. Here's how it works in practice:

**Incident:** A worker fell from a ladder and was injured.
**Why #1:** Why did the worker fall from the ladder?
**Answer:** The ladder slipped.

**Why #2:** Why did the ladder slip?
**Answer:** It wasn't properly secured at the base.

**Why #3:** Why wasn't it properly secured?
**Answer:** The worker was in a hurry and didn't take time to set it up correctly.

**Why #4:** Why was the worker in a hurry?
**Answer:** The supervisor was pressuring the crew to finish the job quickly.

**Why #5:** Why was the supervisor pressuring the crew?
**Answer:** The project was behind schedule, and there were penalties for late completion.

This simple example reveals that the "root cause" isn't the worker's failure to secure the ladder, but organizational pressures that encouraged unsafe shortcuts. Addressing only ladder setup procedures won't prevent similar incidents if the underlying schedule pressures remain.

The 5 Whys technique is particularly useful for relatively simple incidents or as a starting point for more complex investigations. However, it can oversimplify situations where multiple factors contribute to an incident.

## Fault Tree Analysis

Fault Tree Analysis (FTA) is a systematic, top-down approach that maps out all the potential causes and contributing factors that could lead to a specific incident. It's particularly useful for complex incidents with multiple contributing factors.

The process starts with the incident (the "top event") and works backward to identify all the possible pathways that could lead to that outcome. Each pathway is broken down into its contributing factors using logical gates (AND, OR) to show how different factors combine to create the conditions for the incident.

For example, a crane accident might require both mechanical failure AND inadequate inspection procedures to occur. The fault tree would map out all the ways mechanical failure could happen (wear, improper maintenance, manufacturing defects) and all the ways inspection procedures could be inadequate (untrained inspectors, missing checklists, time pressures).

FTA is excellent for complex incidents but can be time-consuming and may require specialized training to use effectively. It's most appropriate for serious incidents or when you need to thoroughly understand all possible failure modes in a system.

## Barrier Analysis

Barrier Analysis focuses on the barriers (controls) that should prevent incidents and examines why those barriers failed. This approach is particularly useful because it directly identifies opportunities for improvement.

Every workplace has multiple barriers designed to prevent incidents:
- **Physical barriers:** Guardrails, machine guards, personal protective equipment

- **Administrative barriers:** Procedures, training, supervision, permits
- **Human barriers:** Skills, knowledge, awareness, motivation

When an incident occurs, one or more of these barriers failed. Barrier Analysis systematically examines each barrier to understand:
- Was the barrier present?
- Was it adequate for the hazard?
- Why did it fail?
- How can it be strengthened?

This approach is particularly valuable because it directly points toward corrective actions. If a physical barrier failed, you might need better equipment or design. If an administrative barrier failed, you might need improved procedures or training.

## Timeline Analysis

Timeline Analysis reconstructs the sequence of events leading up to and during an incident. This chronological approach helps identify critical decision points and reveals how seemingly minor events can combine to create dangerous situations.

The process involves:
1. Establishing a baseline of normal operations
2. Identifying when things began to deviate from normal
3. Mapping the sequence of events, decisions, and conditions
4. Identifying critical moments where different actions could have prevented the incident

Timeline Analysis is particularly useful for incidents that

unfold over time rather than single-moment failures. It's also valuable for understanding how organizational and environmental factors contributed to the incident.

### Change Analysis

Change Analysis examines what was different about the situation when the incident occurred compared to when the same work was performed safely. This approach recognizes that incidents often occur when something changes in the work environment, procedures, personnel, or conditions.

The investigation asks:
- What was different about this job compared to similar jobs performed safely?
- What had changed recently in procedures, equipment, personnel, or conditions?
- How did these changes contribute to the incident?

Change Analysis is particularly effective because it focuses attention on the specific factors that created the incident conditions. It's also relatively quick and straightforward to apply.

## Evidence Collection and Preservation

The quality of your investigation depends heavily on the evidence you collect. Once an incident scene is disturbed or witnesses have time to reconsider their accounts, valuable information may be lost forever. Systematic evidence collection is crucial for understanding what really happened.

### Immediate Scene Preservation

When you arrive at an incident scene, your first priority is ensuring that injured workers receive appropriate medical attention. Once that's addressed, focus on preserving the scene in its post-incident state as much as possible.

Take photographs from multiple angles before anything is moved. Document the position of equipment, materials, and any other relevant items. If the scene must be disturbed for safety reasons or to continue operations, document the original conditions as thoroughly as possible first.

Remember that the "scene" may extend beyond the immediate area where the incident occurred. If a crane accident happened, the scene might include the maintenance shop where the crane was last serviced, the staging area where loads were prepared, and the office where lift plans were developed.

**Physical Evidence**
Physical evidence includes anything tangible that might provide information about the incident:

**Equipment and Tools:** Examine all equipment involved in the incident. Look for signs of wear, damage, modification, or improper use. Document the condition of safety devices, guards, and controls. For mechanical failures, preserve failed components for detailed analysis.

**Materials and Substances:** Collect samples of materials involved in the incident. This might include concrete that failed, chemicals that were being used, or soil from an excavation collapse. Handle and store samples properly to maintain their integrity.

**Environmental Conditions:** Document weather conditions, lighting, noise levels, and any other environmental factors that might have contributed to the incident. These conditions may change quickly, so record them as soon as possible.

**Personal Protective Equipment:** Examine all PPE worn by workers involved in the incident. Document its condition, proper fit, and any signs of impact or failure. PPE can provide valuable clues about the forces involved in an incident and whether it performed as expected.

### Documentary Evidence
Written records can provide crucial information about the circumstances leading up to an incident:

**Work Orders and Job Plans:** Review the planned approach to the work and any changes that were made. Look for conflicts between different documents or unrealistic expectations.

**Training Records:** Verify that workers involved in the incident had received appropriate training for their tasks. Look for gaps in training or recent changes in procedures that might not have been adequately communicated.

**Inspection and Maintenance Records:** Examine records for equipment involved in the incident. Look for patterns of problems, missed inspections, or deferred maintenance.

**Communication Records:** Review emails, text messages, phone logs, and other communications related to the work. These can reveal pressures, concerns, or information that might not emerge in interviews.

**Previous Incident Reports:** Look for similar incidents or near-misses that might indicate ongoing problems or trends.

### Digital Evidence
Modern construction sites generate enormous amounts of digital data that can be valuable for incident investigations:

**Security Camera Footage:** Video evidence can be invaluable for understanding exactly what happened. Act quickly to preserve footage before it's overwritten.

**Equipment Data Logs:** Many modern machines maintain electronic logs of their operation, including speed, load, and operator inputs. This data can provide objective information about equipment performance during an incident.

**GPS and Telematics Data:** Fleet management systems can provide information about vehicle location, speed, and operation patterns that might be relevant to incidents.

**Digital Photos and Videos:** Workers increasingly document their work with smartphones. These images might provide information about conditions before an incident occurred.

## Interview Techniques and Best Practices

Witness interviews are often the most valuable source of information in incident investigations, but they're also the most challenging to conduct effectively. People's memories are influenced by stress, expectations, and social pressures. Skilled interviewing techniques can help you gather accurate, complete information while maintaining positive relationships with workers.

### Preparing for Interviews

Before conducting interviews, gather as much background information as possible. Review available physical evidence, documents, and preliminary reports. This preparation helps you ask informed questions and identify inconsistencies in accounts.

Plan your interview strategy carefully. Decide who to interview and in what order. Generally, it's best to interview witnesses with the most direct knowledge first and save supervisors and managers for later, after you understand the basic facts.

Consider the timing of interviews carefully. People's memories are most accurate immediately after an event, but they may also be most stressed and emotional. Sometimes it's better to wait a day or two for people to process the experience, but don't wait so long that memories fade or become influenced by discussions with others.

## Creating the Right Environment

The setting and tone of your interviews significantly impact the quality of information you receive. Choose a private, comfortable location where the interviewee won't be interrupted or overheard by coworkers or supervisors.

Begin each interview by explaining the purpose of the investigation and emphasizing that the goal is learning and prevention, not blame assignment. Be clear about who will have access to the information and how it will be used.

Establish rapport with the interviewee before diving into the incident details. Ask about their background, experience, and role in the work. This helps them feel more comfortable and provides context for their account of the incident.

## Effective Questioning Techniques

Use open-ended questions that encourage detailed responses rather than yes/no answers. Instead of asking "Did you see the ladder fall?" ask "Tell me what you observed when the incident occurred."

Follow a logical sequence in your questioning:
1. **Background:** Establish the person's role, experience, and normal responsibilities
2. **Pre-incident:** Understand the conditions and activities leading up to the incident

3. **Incident:** Get a detailed account of what happened during the incident
4. **Post-incident:** Understand the immediate response and any relevant observations

Use the "funnel" technique: start with broad, general questions and gradually narrow down to specific details. This approach helps people organize their thoughts and provides a natural flow to the conversation.

Avoid leading questions that suggest a particular answer. Instead of asking "The ladder wasn't properly secured, was it?" ask "How was the ladder positioned?"
Use silence effectively. After asking a question, give the person time to think and respond fully. Don't rush to fill uncomfortable silences - people often provide their most valuable information after a pause.

## Handling Difficult Situations
Some interviews will be challenging due to the emotional state of the interviewee, concerns about consequences, or conflicting accounts of events.

**Emotional Responses:** If someone becomes upset during an interview, acknowledge their feelings and offer to take a break. Don't try to rush through emotional responses - they often contain important information about the human factors involved in the incident.

**Fear of Consequences:** Workers may be reluctant to share information if they fear punishment for themselves or their coworkers. Reiterate the learning purpose of the investigation and be honest about what you can and cannot promise regarding consequences.

**Conflicting Accounts:** When different people provide conflicting information, avoid confronting them directly. Instead, ask follow-up questions to understand their perspective better. Sometimes apparent conflicts resolve when you understand the different vantage points or experiences of the witnesses.

**Reluctant Witnesses:** Some people may be hesitant to participate in interviews. Explain the importance of their perspective and how their information could help prevent future incidents. Be patient and professional, but also be clear about the expectation that they participate in the investigation.

### Documenting Interview Information

Take detailed notes during interviews, but don't let note-taking interfere with the conversation. Consider using audio recording if the interviewee consents, but always take written notes as backup.

Immediately after each interview, review and expand your notes while the conversation is fresh in your memory. Look for themes, patterns, and areas that need follow-up investigation.

Consider having the interviewee review and sign their statement, especially for serious incidents. This ensures accuracy and provides a record that the person had an opportunity to correct any misunderstandings.

## Root Cause Analysis Techniques

Root cause analysis goes beyond identifying what happened to understand why it happened. The goal is to identify the underlying organizational, systemic, and cultural factors that created the conditions for the incident. This deeper understanding is essential for developing effective corrective actions.

## Moving Beyond Human Error

Traditional accident investigations often conclude that "human error" was the root cause. While people do make mistakes, this conclusion is rarely useful for prevention.

Instead of stopping at human error, ask why the error occurred:
- Was the person properly trained for the task?
- Were they provided with adequate tools and equipment?
- Were they under time pressure or other stress?
- Was the procedure clear and realistic?
- Had they seen others perform the task differently?
- Were there conflicting priorities or instructions?

These deeper questions reveal the organizational and systemic factors that contributed to the human error. Addressing these underlying issues is more effective than simply telling people to "be more careful."

## The Swiss Cheese Model

James Reason's Swiss Cheese Model provides a useful framework for understanding how incidents occur in complex systems. The model suggests that organizations have multiple layers of protection (like slices of Swiss cheese) designed to prevent incidents. Each layer has holes (weaknesses), but normally these holes don't align.

An incident occurs when the holes in multiple layers align, creating a pathway for the hazard to reach the worker. The investigation should identify:
- Which protective layers failed
- Why each layer had weaknesses
- How the weaknesses aligned to create the incident

conditions
- How to strengthen each layer to prevent future alignment

This model helps investigators think systematically about all the factors that contributed to an incident and avoid focusing too narrowly on the immediate causes.

## Contributing Factors Analysis

Most incidents result from a combination of factors rather than a single cause. Contributing factors analysis systematically examines all the elements that played a role in creating the incident conditions.

**Immediate Causes:** These are the direct causes of the incident - the unsafe acts and unsafe conditions that immediately preceded the event.

**Basic Causes:** These are the underlying reasons why the immediate causes existed. They often involve inadequate management systems, standards, or compliance.

**Root Causes:** These are the fundamental organizational and cultural issues that allowed the basic causes to exist. They often involve leadership decisions, resource allocation, or organizational priorities.

For example:
- **Immediate Cause:** Worker didn't use fall protection
- **Basic Cause:** Fall protection equipment wasn't available at the work location
- **Root Cause:** The organization didn't have adequate systems for ensuring PPE availability

## Organizational Factors

Modern incident investigation recognizes that organizational factors often play a crucial role in creating incident conditions. These factors include:

**Management Systems:** Are policies and procedures adequate, current, and effectively implemented? Do management systems provide clear guidance for the work being performed?

**Training and Competency:** Do workers have the knowledge and skills needed to perform their work safely? Are training programs effective and regularly updated?

**Communication:** Is safety information effectively communicated throughout the organization? Do workers feel comfortable reporting hazards and concerns?

**Resources:** Are adequate resources (time, equipment, personnel) provided for safe work performance? Do resource constraints create pressure for unsafe shortcuts?

**Culture:** What messages does the organization really send about safety priorities? How does the organization respond to safety concerns and incidents?

**Leadership:** Do leaders demonstrate genuine commitment to safety through their actions and decisions? Are safety responsibilities clearly defined and accountability systems effective?

# Corrective Action Development and Tracking

The value of any incident investigation lies in the corrective actions it generates. Without effective follow-through, even the most thorough investigation is merely an academic exercise. This section will help you develop meaningful corrective actions and implement systems to ensure they're completed effectively.

## The Hierarchy of Controls in Corrective Actions

Not all corrective actions are equally effective. The hierarchy of controls provides a framework for developing the most effective solutions to the problems identified in your investigation.

**Elimination:** Can the hazard be completely removed? This is the most effective approach but often the most difficult to implement. For example, if workers are injured by a particular piece of equipment, can the work be redesigned to eliminate the need for that equipment?

**Substitution:** Can the hazard be replaced with something less dangerous? This might involve using different materials, equipment, or methods. For example, substituting a less toxic chemical for a more dangerous one.

**Engineering Controls:** Can physical changes to the workplace or equipment reduce the risk? These might include guardrails, ventilation systems, machine guards, or equipment modifications.

**Administrative Controls:** Can policies, procedures, training, or supervision be improved to reduce risk? While these controls depend on human behavior, they're often necessary supplements to higher-level controls.

**Personal Protective Equipment:** Can PPE provide protection when other controls aren't feasible? PPE should be the last line of defense, not the primary strategy for risk reduction.

When developing corrective actions, start at the top of the

hierarchy and work down. Look for opportunities to eliminate or reduce hazards through engineering solutions before relying on administrative controls or PPE.

## Characteristics of Effective Corrective Actions

**Specific:** Corrective actions should clearly describe what will be done, who will do it, and when it will be completed. Vague statements like "improve training" are not actionable.

**Measurable:** You should be able to determine whether the corrective action has been completed and whether it's achieving the desired results.

**Achievable:** Corrective actions should be realistic given available resources and organizational capabilities. Overly ambitious actions are unlikely to be completed.

**Relevant:** Each corrective action should directly address one or more of the root causes identified in the investigation. If you can't explain how an action will prevent recurrence, it probably isn't necessary.

**Time-bound:** Every corrective action should have a specific completion date. Without deadlines, important actions may be indefinitely postponed.

## Types of Corrective Actions

**Immediate Actions:** These address urgent safety concerns that could result in additional incidents. They're typically implemented within hours or days of the incident and often involve temporary measures while permanent solutions are developed.

**Short-term Actions:** These address specific deficiencies identified in the investigation and can typically be implemented within weeks or months. Examples might include equipment repairs, procedure updates, or additional training.

**Long-term Actions:** These address systemic issues and may require significant time and resources to implement. Examples might include equipment replacement, facility modifications, or major organizational changes.

**Verification Actions:** These ensure that corrective actions are working as intended. They might include follow-up inspections, audits, or reviews to confirm that changes have been effective.

## Implementation and Tracking Systems

Developing good corrective actions is only half the battle - ensuring they're implemented effectively is equally important. Many organizations struggle with corrective action follow-through, leading to repeated incidents from the same causes.

**Assignment of Responsibility:** Each corrective action should be assigned to a specific person who has the authority and resources needed to complete it. Avoid assigning actions to committees or departments without clear individual accountability.

**Regular Review and Updates:** Establish a regular schedule for reviewing the status of corrective actions. Monthly reviews are typically appropriate for most actions, with more frequent reviews for urgent items.

**Escalation Procedures:** Define what happens when corrective actions aren't completed on schedule. This might involve notification of higher management, reallocation of resources, or revision of the action plan.

**Documentation Systems:** Maintain detailed records of all corrective actions, including their status, any obstacles encountered, and evidence of completion. This documentation is valuable for demonstrating due diligence and for future reference.

**Effectiveness Monitoring:** Don't assume that completed corrective actions are effective. Monitor leading and lagging indicators to confirm that the actions are achieving their intended results.

## Common Pitfalls in Corrective Action Development

**Focusing on Symptoms Rather Than Causes:** If your investigation identified that workers weren't using PPE, requiring more PPE training might address the symptom but not the underlying cause. Perhaps the PPE was uncomfortable, unavailable, or workers saw supervisors not using it.

**Over-reliance on Training:** Training is often necessary but rarely sufficient. If people knew what to do but didn't do it, more training probably won't solve the problem. Look for systemic issues that prevented people from following safe practices.

**Punitive Actions Disguised as Corrective Actions:** Disciplinary actions may be appropriate in some cases, but they don't qualify as corrective actions for incident prevention. Focus on changes that will prevent future incidents rather than punishing past behavior.

**Generic Solutions:** Avoid one-size-fits-all corrective actions that don't address the specific circumstances of your incident. Generic solutions are often ineffective because they don't address the actual root causes.

**Unrealistic Expectations:** Don't expect corrective actions to solve complex problems overnight. Systemic issues may require sustained effort over months or years to address effectively.

# Building Investigation Skills and Competency

Effective incident investigation requires a combination of technical knowledge, analytical skills, and interpersonal abilities. These skills can be developed through training, practice, and mentorship, but they require ongoing attention and refinement throughout your career.

### Developing Technical Knowledge

**Understanding Construction Processes:** You can't investigate what you don't understand. Develop a thorough knowledge of construction methods, equipment, and hazards. This knowledge helps you ask the right questions and recognize when something isn't normal.

**Regulatory Requirements:** Stay current with OSHA standards and other applicable regulations. Understanding what's required helps you identify deficiencies and develop appropriate corrective actions.

**Investigation Methodologies:** Study different investigation approaches and practice applying them to various scenarios. No single method works for every situation, so you need a toolkit of approaches.

**Evidence Collection:** Learn proper techniques for photographing scenes, collecting physical evidence, and preserving documentation. Poor evidence collection can undermine even the best analytical work.

## Analytical Skills Development
**Critical Thinking:** Practice questioning assumptions and looking beyond obvious explanations. Ask "what if" questions and consider alternative explanations for the evidence you observe.

**Pattern Recognition:** Learn to identify recurring themes and patterns across multiple incidents. This skill helps you recognize systemic issues that might not be apparent from individual investigations.

**Systems Thinking:** Develop the ability to see how different parts of the organization interact and influence each other. Incidents often result from the interaction of multiple systems rather than failure of a single component.

**Data Analysis:** Learn to work with quantitative data to identify trends and patterns. Statistical analysis can reveal insights that aren't apparent from individual case studies.

## Interpersonal Skills
**Communication:** Develop the ability to communicate with people at all levels of the organization, from entry-level workers to senior executives. Each audience requires a different approach and emphasis.

**Interviewing:** Practice active listening techniques and learn to ask questions that elicit detailed, accurate information without making people defensive.

**Conflict Resolution:** Investigations sometimes reveal conflicts between different groups or individuals. Learn to navigate these situations professionally while maintaining focus on the investigation goals.

**Cultural Sensitivity:** In diverse workplaces, understand how cultural differences might affect people's willingness to share information or their interpretation of events.

## Continuing Education and Professional Development

**Professional Organizations:** Join organizations like the American Society of Safety Professionals (ASSP) or the National Safety Council to access training resources and network with other investigators.

**Training Programs:** Attend formal training programs on investigation techniques, root cause analysis, and related topics. Many organizations offer specialized courses for construction safety professionals.

**Conferences and Seminars:** Participate in industry conferences where you can learn about new investigation techniques and hear case studies from other professionals.

**Mentorship:** Seek out experienced investigators who can provide guidance and feedback on your developing skills. Consider both formal mentoring relationships and informal learning opportunities.

**Case Study Review:** Study well-documented investigation reports from other organizations. Pay attention to the techniques used and the lessons learned.

Incident investigation is one of the most important skills you'll develop as a construction safety professional. Every incident provides an opportunity to learn and improve, but only if you approach the investigation with the right mindset, tools, and techniques. Remember that the goal isn't to assign blame but to understand what happened and prevent it from happening again.

The skills covered in this chapter will serve you throughout your career, helping you identify and address the root causes of workplace incidents. As you gain experience, you'll develop your own style and preferences, but the fundamental principles remain the same: be thorough, be objective, and focus on learning and prevention.

In the next chapter, we'll explore how to use the insights gained from incident investigations to develop comprehensive safety management systems that address the organizational and systemic factors that contribute to workplace incidents.

# CHAPTER 13: SAFETY MANAGEMENT SYSTEMS

As you advance in your construction safety career, you'll move beyond managing individual hazards and daily compliance tasks toward developing and implementing comprehensive safety management systems (SMS). These systems represent the backbone of world-class safety performance, transforming safety from a collection of rules and procedures into an integrated, systematic approach that drives continuous improvement and cultural change.

Think of a safety management system as the operating system for your organization's safety efforts. Just as your computer's operating system coordinates all the different programs and functions, an SMS coordinates all safety activities, policies, procedures, and resources to work together seamlessly toward common safety objectives.

## Understanding Safety Management Systems

A safety management system is a systematic approach to managing safety that includes the necessary organizational structures, accountabilities, policies, and procedures. It's not simply a safety program or a collection of safety procedures - it's a comprehensive framework that integrates safety considerations into every aspect of business operations.

The concept emerged from high-reliability industries like aviation and nuclear power, where the consequences of failure are catastrophic. These industries recognized that traditional approaches focusing solely on compliance and individual behavior were insufficient. They needed systems that could identify and address systemic issues before they led to accidents.

In construction, SMS adoption has accelerated as organizations recognize that sustainable safety excellence requires more than good intentions and hard work. It requires systematic management of safety risks, clear accountability structures, and processes that ensure safety considerations are embedded in all business decisions.

## Core Elements of Safety Management Systems

While different SMS frameworks exist, most share four fundamental elements that work together to create a comprehensive safety management approach.

### Policy and Strategic Objectives

The foundation of any SMS is a clear safety policy that establishes the organization's commitment to safety and defines strategic safety objectives. This isn't just a statement hanging on the wall - it's a living document that guides decision-making at all levels.

Effective safety policies articulate the organization's safety vision, establish safety as a core business value, and provide clear direction for safety performance expectations. They assign accountability for safety performance to leadership and establish the framework for continuous improvement.

Your safety policy should be specific enough to provide meaningful guidance but flexible enough to allow for adaptation as your organization grows and changes. It should address key areas such as regulatory compliance, risk management, employee involvement, and continuous improvement commitments.

Strategic safety objectives translate your policy into measurable goals that drive organizational performance. These objectives should be SMART (Specific, Measurable, Achievable, Relevant, Time-bound) and aligned with your organization's business objectives. Examples might include reducing injury rates by a specific percentage, achieving zero fatalities, or improving safety training completion rates.

**Risk Management**

The risk management element focuses on systematic identification, assessment, and control of safety risks throughout your operations. This goes beyond traditional hazard identification to include systematic analysis of how hazards interact with your work processes, organizational factors, and external influences.

Effective risk management starts with comprehensive hazard identification processes that capture not just obvious physical hazards but also organizational and systemic risks. This includes analyzing how work is actually performed versus how it's supposed to be performed, identifying potential failure modes in your safety systems, and understanding how external pressures might compromise safety performance.

Risk assessment within an SMS framework involves evaluating both the likelihood and consequences of potential incidents, but it also considers the effectiveness of existing controls and the organization's capacity to manage different types of risks. This helps prioritize risk control efforts and resource allocation decisions.

Risk control follows the hierarchy of controls but within a systematic framework that considers the interconnections between different hazards and controls. The SMS approach emphasizes designing out hazards through engineering controls and administrative systems rather than relying primarily on personal protective equipment and individual behavior.

**Assurance**
The assurance element ensures that your safety management system is working as intended and identifies opportunities for improvement. This includes both proactive monitoring of system performance and reactive investigation of incidents and near-misses.

Proactive assurance activities include safety audits, inspections, and performance monitoring that assess both compliance with procedures and the effectiveness of safety controls. These activities should be systematic and regular, with clear criteria for evaluation and standardized reporting processes.

Safety performance indicators are crucial for assurance. Leading indicators measure the health of your safety systems and processes, while lagging indicators measure safety outcomes. Effective SMS uses both types of indicators to provide a complete picture of safety performance and identify trends before they result in incidents.

Incident investigation within an SMS framework goes beyond determining immediate causes to identify systemic issues that contributed to incidents. This includes analyzing organizational factors, management system failures, and underlying conditions that allowed hazards to materialize into actual harm.

## Promotion

The promotion element ensures that your organization has the competencies, culture, and communication necessary to support effective safety management. This includes safety training, safety culture development, and communication systems that support safety performance.

Competency management ensures that all personnel have the knowledge, skills, and abilities necessary to perform their safety responsibilities effectively. This includes not just technical safety training but also leadership development, safety management skills, and cultural competencies necessary for effective safety performance.

Safety culture promotion involves creating an environment where safety is valued, supported, and integrated into daily operations. This requires leadership commitment, employee engagement, and systems that encourage reporting, learning, and continuous improvement.

Communication systems ensure that safety information flows effectively throughout the organization and that safety lessons learned are captured and shared. This includes both formal reporting systems and informal communication channels that support safety awareness and performance.

# Performance Measurement and Metrics

Effective SMS requires sophisticated performance measurement systems that provide insights into both safety outcomes and the health of your safety management processes. Traditional safety metrics focused primarily on injury rates, but SMS requires a broader range of indicators that provide early warning of potential problems and measure the effectiveness of your safety systems.

## Leading Indicators

Leading indicators measure the inputs and activities that drive safety performance. These indicators help you understand whether your safety systems are functioning effectively and provide early warning of potential problems before they result in incidents.

Examples of leading indicators include safety training completion rates, hazard identification and correction rates, safety audit scores, near-miss reporting rates, and employee safety perception survey results. These indicators help you manage safety proactively rather than simply reacting to incidents after they occur.

The key to effective leading indicators is ensuring they measure meaningful activities that actually drive safety performance. Simply counting safety activities isn't sufficient - you need to measure the quality and effectiveness of those activities in reducing risk and improving safety performance.

## Lagging Indicators

Lagging indicators measure safety outcomes and results. While these indicators tell you how you've performed in the past, they're essential for understanding the ultimate effectiveness of your safety efforts and identifying areas where improvement is needed.

Traditional lagging indicators include injury rates, illness rates, fatality rates, and workers' compensation costs. However, SMS approaches often include additional lagging indicators such as regulatory citations, safety-related work delays, and customer safety satisfaction ratings.

The challenge with lagging indicators is that they're reactive - they tell you about problems after they've occurred. However, they're essential for validating the effectiveness of your leading indicators and ensuring that your proactive safety efforts are actually producing the desired results.

**Balanced Scorecards**
Many organizations use balanced scorecard approaches that combine leading and lagging indicators across different perspectives to provide a comprehensive view of safety performance. This might include operational indicators (injury rates, audit scores), financial indicators (safety costs, return on safety investment), stakeholder indicators (employee satisfaction, customer confidence), and learning and growth indicators (training completion, safety innovation).

The key is selecting indicators that provide meaningful insights into your safety performance and help drive continuous improvement. Too many indicators can overwhelm decision-makers, while too few may miss important aspects of safety performance.

# Continuous Improvement Processes
Continuous improvement is what transforms an SMS from

a static compliance system into a dynamic, learning organization that constantly adapts and improves its safety performance. This requires systematic processes for identifying improvement opportunities, implementing changes, and measuring their effectiveness.

## Plan-Do-Check-Act Cycles

The Plan-Do-Check-Act (PDCA) cycle provides a systematic framework for continuous improvement within your SMS. This cycle ensures that improvements are planned systematically, implemented effectively, evaluated thoroughly, and standardized when successful.

The Plan phase involves identifying improvement opportunities, analyzing root causes, and developing improvement strategies. This might come from incident investigations, audit findings, performance data analysis, or employee suggestions.

The Do phase involves implementing improvement initiatives on a pilot or small scale to test their effectiveness. This allows you to identify potential problems and refine your approach before full-scale implementation.

The Check phase involves evaluating the effectiveness of your improvement initiatives using both quantitative data and qualitative feedback. This assessment determines whether the changes achieved their intended results and identifies any unintended consequences.

The Act phase involves standardizing successful improvements and incorporating lessons learned into your SMS. This ensures that improvements become permanent parts of your safety management system rather than temporary fixes.

## Management Review

Regular management review is essential for ensuring that your SMS continues to meet your organization's needs and drives continuous improvement. Management reviews should assess the effectiveness of your SMS, identify improvement opportunities, and ensure adequate resources are allocated to safety management.

Effective management reviews examine both safety performance data and the effectiveness of safety management processes. This includes reviewing incident trends, audit findings, performance indicator results, and feedback from stakeholders about the effectiveness of your safety systems.

Management reviews should result in specific decisions about safety objectives, resource allocation, system improvements, and strategic direction. These reviews demonstrate leadership commitment to safety and ensure that safety management remains aligned with business objectives.

## Employee Involvement

Continuous improvement requires the active involvement of employees at all levels. Frontline workers often have the best insights into safety hazards and improvement opportunities, while supervisors and managers can identify systemic issues that affect safety performance.

Effective employee involvement includes formal processes such as safety committees, suggestion systems, and improvement teams, as well as informal processes that encourage open communication about safety issues and ideas for improvement.

The key is creating systems that not only collect employee

input but also respond effectively to their suggestions and feedback. Employees need to see that their input is valued and that it leads to meaningful improvements in safety performance.

# Integration with Quality and Environmental Systems

Modern organizations increasingly recognize that safety, quality, and environmental management are interconnected and benefit from integrated management approaches. Integrated management systems reduce duplication, improve efficiency, and ensure that these critical business functions work together rather than competing for resources and attention.

### Common Elements

Safety, quality, and environmental management systems share many common elements, including policy development, risk management, competency management, document control, internal auditing, and management review. Integrating these common elements reduces administrative burden and ensures consistency across different management systems.

For example, your document control procedures can manage safety, quality, and environmental documents using the same processes and systems. Internal audit programs can assess all three management systems simultaneously, providing a more comprehensive view of organizational performance.

### Synergies and Trade-offs

Integration allows organizations to identify and leverage synergies between safety, quality, and environmental objectives. For example, waste reduction initiatives often improve both environmental performance and workplace safety by reducing exposure to hazardous materials.

However, integration also requires careful management of potential trade-offs between different objectives. Production pressures that compromise safety might also affect quality, while environmental initiatives might introduce new safety hazards that need to be managed.

The key is developing integrated approaches that optimize overall organizational performance rather than optimizing individual functions in isolation. This requires leadership that understands the interconnections between different management systems and makes decisions based on overall organizational objectives.

**Implementation Strategies**
Successful integration requires careful planning and phased implementation. Organizations often start by aligning policies and objectives across different management systems, then gradually integrate processes and procedures where it makes sense.

Training and competency development are crucial for integration success. Managers and supervisors need to understand how safety, quality, and environmental management work together and how to make decisions that optimize overall performance.

Communication systems should also be integrated to ensure that lessons learned in one area are shared across all management systems. This includes incident investigation findings, audit results, and best practices that might be applicable across different functions.

# Building Your SMS Implementation Skills

As a safety professional, you'll likely be involved in developing, implementing, or improving safety management systems throughout your career. This requires specific skills and competencies beyond traditional safety technical knowledge.

## Systems Thinking

SMS requires systems thinking - the ability to understand how different parts of an organization interact and influence each other. This includes understanding how organizational culture, business processes, external pressures, and individual behaviors combine to influence safety performance.

Developing systems thinking skills involves learning to see patterns and relationships rather than just individual events. This includes understanding feedback loops, unintended consequences, and the long-term effects of management decisions on safety performance.

## Change Management

Implementing or improving an SMS involves significant organizational change that requires careful management. This includes understanding how people respond to change, developing strategies to overcome resistance, and ensuring that changes are implemented effectively and sustained over time.

Change management skills include stakeholder analysis, communication planning, training design, and implementation project management. These skills are essential for ensuring that SMS improvements are successful and sustainable.

### Data Analysis

Modern SMS generates large amounts of data that must be analyzed effectively to drive improvement. This requires skills in statistical analysis, trend identification, and data visualization that help translate raw data into actionable insights.

You don't need to become a statistician, but you should understand basic statistical concepts and know how to use data analysis tools to identify patterns and trends in safety performance data.

## Common Implementation Challenges

Understanding common SMS implementation challenges can help you avoid pitfalls and develop more effective implementation strategies.

### Leadership Commitment

SMS requires sustained leadership commitment that goes beyond initial enthusiasm. Leaders must be willing to invest resources, make difficult decisions, and maintain focus on safety even when facing competing business pressures.

Building and maintaining leadership commitment requires demonstrating the business value of SMS, providing regular feedback on system performance, and ensuring that leaders have the information and support they need to make effective safety decisions.

### Cultural Resistance

Organizations with traditional safety cultures may resist SMS approaches that require greater employee involvement, transparency, and systematic thinking. Overcoming this resistance requires patient culture change efforts that demonstrate the benefits of SMS approaches.

Cultural change strategies include leadership modeling, employee engagement, communication campaigns, and recognition programs that reinforce desired behaviors and attitudes.

### Resource Constraints

SMS implementation requires significant resources for system development, training, technology, and ongoing maintenance. Organizations may underestimate these resource requirements or fail to sustain resource commitments over time.

Effective resource management requires careful planning, phased implementation approaches, and clear demonstration of return on investment to maintain organizational support for SMS initiatives.

### Complexity Management

SMS can become overly complex and bureaucratic if not carefully managed. The goal is systematic management, not unnecessarily complicated processes that interfere with productive work.

Managing complexity requires focusing on essential elements, continuous simplification efforts, and regular review of system effectiveness to ensure that SMS supports rather than hinders organizational performance.

## Your Role in SMS Development

As you advance in your safety career, you'll likely play increasingly important roles in SMS development and implementation. Understanding these roles can help you prepare for advancement opportunities and contribute more effectively to organizational safety performance.

### Technical Expertise
You'll need deep technical knowledge of SMS frameworks, implementation strategies, and best practices. This includes understanding different SMS standards (such as ISO 45001), industry-specific guidance, and emerging trends in safety management.

Developing this expertise requires continuous learning through professional development programs, industry conferences, and networking with other SMS practitioners.

### Change Leadership
SMS implementation requires change leadership skills that help organizations navigate the cultural and operational changes necessary for effective safety management. This includes stakeholder engagement, communication, and project management skills.

### Strategic Thinking
Advanced SMS roles require strategic thinking abilities that help align safety management with business objectives and identify opportunities for competitive advantage through superior safety performance.

This includes understanding business strategy, financial management, and organizational development concepts that help you contribute to broader organizational success while advancing safety objectives.

## Looking Forward
Safety management systems represent the future of construction safety management. As the industry continues to evolve, organizations that adopt systematic approaches

to safety management will have significant advantages in attracting and retaining talent, winning contracts, and achieving sustainable business success.

Your role as a safety professional is to help your organization develop and implement SMS approaches that drive continuous improvement in safety performance while supporting business objectives. This requires technical expertise, change leadership skills, and strategic thinking that goes beyond traditional safety management approaches.

The investment in developing SMS capabilities pays dividends throughout your career as organizations increasingly recognize that systematic safety management is essential for sustainable business success. By developing these capabilities early in your career, you position yourself for advancement opportunities and the satisfaction of making meaningful contributions to worker safety and organizational performance.

In our next chapter, we'll explore emerging trends and technologies that are transforming construction safety, including how digital tools and artificial intelligence are being integrated into modern safety management systems to drive even greater improvements in safety performance.

# CHAPTER 14: EMERGING TRENDS AND TECHNOLOGIES

The construction industry is experiencing a technological revolution that's fundamentally changing how we approach safety management. As a safety professional entering this field, understanding these emerging trends and technologies isn't just about staying current - it's about positioning yourself at the forefront of an industry transformation that will define the next generation of construction safety practice.

The digital transformation of construction safety represents one of the most significant shifts in the industry since the introduction of modern safety regulations. While construction has traditionally been slow to adopt new technologies, the combination of improved technology capabilities, cost reductions, and demonstrated safety benefits is driving rapid adoption across the industry.

These technologies aren't replacing traditional safety approaches - they're enhancing and amplifying them. The fundamental principles of hazard recognition, risk assessment, and control implementation remain the same, but new technologies are making these processes more efficient, more accurate, and more effective than ever before.

Understanding and leveraging these technologies will be essential for your success as a construction safety professional. Organizations are increasingly looking for safety professionals who can bridge the gap between traditional safety knowledge and emerging technological capabilities.

# Digital Safety Tools and Mobile Applications

The proliferation of smartphones and tablets on construction sites has created unprecedented opportunities for digital safety tools that put powerful safety management capabilities directly into the hands of workers and supervisors. These tools are transforming how safety information is collected, analyzed, and acted upon.

### Mobile Safety Management Platforms

Comprehensive mobile safety management platforms are replacing paper-based safety systems with integrated digital solutions that streamline safety processes while improving data quality and accessibility. These platforms typically include modules for incident reporting, hazard identification, inspection management, training tracking, and communication.

The advantages of mobile platforms extend beyond simple digitization. Real-time data synchronization means that safety information is immediately available to all stakeholders, enabling faster response to safety issues. GPS and timestamp capabilities provide accurate location and timing data that improves investigation quality and trend analysis.

Photo and video capture capabilities built into mobile devices allow for rich documentation of safety conditions, incidents, and corrective actions. This visual documentation improves communication quality and provides valuable evidence for investigations and training purposes.

Many platforms include offline capabilities that allow safety data collection to continue even when internet connectivity is limited or unavailable. Data is automatically synchronized when connectivity is restored, ensuring that no safety information is lost due to technical limitations.

Integration capabilities allow mobile safety platforms to connect with other business systems such as project management software, enterprise resource planning systems, and human resources databases. This integration eliminates duplicate data entry and ensures that safety information is available where business decisions are made.

**Specialized Safety Applications**

Beyond comprehensive platforms, numerous specialized applications address specific safety functions or hazards. These applications often provide deeper functionality in specific areas while maintaining ease of use and affordability for smaller organizations.

Fall protection applications help users select appropriate fall protection systems, calculate anchor point requirements, and verify compliance with regulations. Some applications include augmented reality features that allow users to visualize fall hazards and protection systems on actual job sites.

Electrical safety applications provide guidance on lockout/tagout procedures, arc flash analysis, and electrical hazard assessment. These applications often include reference materials, calculation tools, and documentation capabilities that support electrical safety programs.

Chemical safety applications help users access safety data sheets, perform exposure assessments, and select appropriate personal protective equipment. Some applications include barcode scanning capabilities that automatically retrieve chemical information and provide instant access to safety data.

Emergency response applications provide digital access to emergency procedures, contact information, and site-specific emergency plans. GPS capabilities can automatically determine user location and provide location-specific emergency information.

## Data Collection and Analytics

Mobile applications are generating unprecedented amounts of safety data that provide new insights into safety performance and improvement opportunities. This data goes far beyond traditional injury statistics to include near-miss events, hazard observations, behavioral observations, and environmental conditions.

Advanced analytics capabilities built into modern safety applications can identify patterns and trends that would be impossible to detect through manual analysis. Machine learning algorithms can analyze historical data to predict future safety risks and recommend preventive actions.

Real-time dashboards provide immediate visibility into safety performance across multiple projects and locations. These dashboards can highlight emerging issues, track corrective action completion, and provide early warning of potential problems.

Integration with other data sources such as weather services, project schedules, and equipment monitoring systems provides a more complete picture of factors that influence safety performance. This integrated data analysis can reveal correlations and causation relationships that inform more effective safety management strategies.

## Wearable Technology and IoT in Safety

The Internet of Things (IoT) and wearable technology are creating new possibilities for real-time safety monitoring and intervention. These technologies can detect dangerous conditions, monitor worker behavior, and provide immediate alerts when safety risks are identified.

### Personal Monitoring Devices

Wearable devices designed for construction workers can monitor a wide range of safety-related parameters including location, movement patterns, environmental conditions, and physiological indicators. This continuous monitoring provides unprecedented visibility into worker safety status and exposure levels.

Smart hard hats equipped with sensors can detect impacts, monitor environmental conditions such as temperature and air quality, and provide communication capabilities. Some models include proximity sensors that alert workers when they're approaching dangerous areas or equipment.

Wearable air quality monitors can detect exposure to hazardous gases, particulates, and other airborne contaminants. These devices provide real-time exposure data and can trigger immediate alerts when exposure limits are approached or exceeded.

Personal fall detection devices can automatically detect

when a worker has fallen and trigger emergency response procedures. These devices are particularly valuable for workers who work alone or in remote areas where falls might not be immediately noticed.

Fatigue monitoring devices use various physiological indicators to assess worker alertness and fatigue levels. These devices can alert supervisors when workers may be too fatigued to work safely and help optimize work schedules to reduce fatigue-related risks.

**Environmental Monitoring Systems**
IoT-enabled environmental monitoring systems provide continuous monitoring of job site conditions that affect worker safety. These systems can detect changes in air quality, noise levels, temperature, humidity, and other environmental factors that influence safety performance.

Wireless sensor networks can monitor large job sites with minimal infrastructure requirements. Solar-powered sensors can operate independently for extended periods while providing continuous data transmission to safety management systems.
Integration with weather services and forecasting systems allows environmental monitoring systems to predict changing conditions and provide advance warning of potential safety hazards such as severe weather, temperature extremes, or air quality issues.

Automated alert systems can notify safety personnel immediately when environmental conditions exceed preset thresholds. These alerts can trigger immediate protective actions such as work stoppages, shelter procedures, or equipment shutdowns.

## Equipment and Vehicle Monitoring
IoT sensors on construction equipment and vehicles provide real-time monitoring of operating conditions, maintenance status, and safety system performance. This monitoring can prevent equipment-related accidents by identifying problems before they result in failures.

Proximity detection systems can prevent collisions between equipment and workers by automatically slowing or stopping equipment when workers are detected in danger zones. These systems are particularly valuable for large equipment operators who may have limited visibility.

Operator monitoring systems can assess equipment operator alertness, competency, and compliance with safety procedures. These systems can provide immediate feedback to operators and alert supervisors when safety protocols are not being followed.
Predictive maintenance systems use sensor data and machine learning algorithms to predict when equipment maintenance is needed before failures occur. This predictive approach prevents safety hazards associated with equipment failures while reducing maintenance costs.

## Data Integration and Analysis
The value of wearable technology and IoT systems is maximized when data from multiple sources is integrated and analyzed to provide comprehensive insights into safety performance. This integration requires sophisticated data management and analysis capabilities.

Real-time data processing allows for immediate response to safety risks detected by monitoring systems. Machine learning algorithms can analyze patterns in sensor data to identify emerging risks before they result in incidents.

Predictive analytics can use historical sensor data combined with other factors such as weather conditions, work schedules, and project phases to predict when and where safety risks are most likely to occur. This predictive capability allows for proactive risk management rather than reactive response.

Integration with safety management systems ensures that data from wearable devices and IoT sensors is incorporated into broader safety management processes including incident investigation, trend analysis, and performance measurement.

# Virtual and Augmented Reality for Training

Virtual Reality (VR) and Augmented Reality (AR) technologies are revolutionizing safety training by providing immersive, realistic training experiences that allow workers to practice safety procedures and experience hazardous situations without actual risk.

**Virtual Reality Safety Training**

VR safety training creates completely immersive virtual environments where workers can experience realistic construction scenarios and practice safety procedures. These virtual environments can simulate dangerous situations that would be impossible or too risky to replicate in traditional training settings.

Fall protection training using VR allows workers to experience working at height and practice fall protection procedures in a safe virtual environment. Workers can experience the consequences of safety failures without physical risk, creating powerful learning experiences that reinforce the importance of proper procedures.

Confined space training in virtual environments allows workers to practice entry procedures, atmospheric monitoring, and emergency response in realistic confined spaces without the risks associated with actual confined space training.

Electrical safety training using VR can simulate electrical hazards, arc flash events, and lockout/tagout procedures in ways that demonstrate the consequences of electrical accidents without exposing trainees to actual electrical hazards.

Equipment operation training in virtual environments allows operators to practice with realistic equipment controls and responses while learning to recognize and respond to potential safety hazards. This training can be particularly valuable for expensive or specialized equipment where hands-on training opportunities are limited.

**Augmented Reality Applications**
AR technology overlays digital information onto real-world environments, providing contextual safety information and guidance directly in workers' field of view. This technology is particularly valuable for complex procedures and hazard recognition training.

Safety procedure guidance using AR can provide step-by-step visual instructions for complex safety procedures such as scaffold erection, fall protection system installation, or hazardous material handling. These visual guides can reduce errors and improve procedure compliance.

Hazard visualization using AR can highlight potential hazards that might not be immediately visible to workers. For example, AR applications can show the location of buried utilities, highlight fall hazards, or indicate areas with potential chemical exposures.

Personal protective equipment training using AR can demonstrate proper selection, use, and maintenance of PPE while showing the consequences of improper use. This visual demonstration can be more effective than traditional classroom training.

Equipment inspection training using AR can guide workers through inspection procedures by highlighting inspection points and providing visual indicators of acceptable and unacceptable conditions.

**Training Effectiveness and Measurement**
VR and AR training platforms provide unprecedented capabilities for measuring training effectiveness and ensuring that learning objectives are achieved. These platforms can track trainee performance, identify areas where additional training is needed, and verify competency achievement.

Performance analytics built into VR training systems can measure reaction times, decision quality, procedure compliance, and other indicators of training effectiveness. This data can be used to customize training experiences for individual learners and identify areas where training programs need improvement.

Competency verification using VR simulations can provide objective assessment of worker abilities to perform safety procedures correctly under various conditions. This verification can be more comprehensive and reliable than traditional testing methods.

Training standardization is enhanced by VR and AR systems that provide identical training experiences regardless of location or instructor. This standardization ensures that all workers receive consistent, high-quality safety training.

Cost-effectiveness of VR and AR training improves over time as the technology costs decrease while training quality and effectiveness increase. Organizations can provide high-quality safety training without the costs and risks associated with creating realistic training scenarios in the physical world.

# Artificial Intelligence in Hazard Prediction

Artificial Intelligence (AI) and machine learning are beginning to transform construction safety by providing capabilities to predict and prevent safety incidents before they occur. These technologies analyze vast amounts of data to identify patterns and relationships that human analysis might miss.

### Predictive Analytics for Safety

AI-powered predictive analytics systems analyze historical safety data, project characteristics, weather conditions, work schedules, and other factors to identify when and where safety incidents are most likely to occur. This predictive capability allows for proactive risk management and resource allocation.

Incident prediction models can analyze patterns in near-miss reports, environmental conditions, work pressures, and other factors to predict when incidents are most likely to occur. These predictions allow safety managers to implement additional controls or modify work procedures before incidents happen.

Resource allocation optimization using AI can help

organizations deploy safety resources where they're most needed. AI systems can analyze multiple projects simultaneously to identify which locations require additional safety attention and recommend optimal resource deployment strategies.

Risk scoring systems powered by AI can automatically assess and rank safety risks based on multiple factors including historical data, current conditions, and predictive models. These risk scores help prioritize safety interventions and resource allocation decisions.

Trend analysis using machine learning can identify subtle patterns in safety data that might not be apparent through traditional analysis methods. These patterns can reveal emerging risks or the effectiveness of safety interventions over time.

## Computer Vision for Hazard Detection

Computer vision technology uses cameras and AI algorithms to automatically detect safety hazards and unsafe behaviors on construction sites. This technology provides continuous monitoring capabilities that supplement human observation and inspection.

Personal protective equipment compliance monitoring using computer vision can automatically verify that workers are wearing required PPE and alert supervisors when non-compliance is detected. These systems can monitor large areas continuously without requiring dedicated personnel.

Unsafe behavior detection systems can identify behaviors such as working without fall protection, entering restricted areas, or using equipment improperly. These systems can provide immediate alerts that allow for rapid intervention.

Equipment safety monitoring using computer vision can detect when equipment is operating unsafely, when safety devices are not functioning properly, or when equipment is being used outside of safe operating parameters.

Housekeeping and site condition monitoring can automatically identify housekeeping issues, blocked egress routes, unstable materials, and other environmental hazards that affect worker safety.

**Natural Language Processing**
Natural Language Processing (NLP) technology can analyze text-based safety data such as incident reports, inspection findings, and worker feedback to identify patterns and extract insights that inform safety decision-making.

Incident report analysis using NLP can automatically categorize incidents, identify contributing factors, and suggest corrective actions based on analysis of large numbers of similar incidents. This analysis can reveal patterns that might not be apparent through manual review.

Safety communication analysis can evaluate the effectiveness of safety communications by analyzing worker feedback, question patterns, and comprehension indicators. This analysis can help improve safety communication strategies and materials.

Regulatory compliance monitoring using NLP can automatically scan safety documentation, procedures, and communications to identify potential compliance issues and ensure that safety programs meet regulatory requirements.

Knowledge extraction from safety documents can automatically identify best practices, lessons learned, and critical safety information from large volumes of safety documentation, making this knowledge more accessible and actionable.

**Integration and Implementation Considerations**
Successful implementation of AI in construction safety requires careful consideration of data quality, system integration, user acceptance, and ethical implications.

Data quality is critical for AI system effectiveness. Poor quality data will produce poor quality predictions and recommendations. Organizations must invest in data management capabilities and ensure that AI systems have access to accurate, complete, and timely data.

System integration is essential for maximizing AI value. AI systems must integrate with existing safety management systems, project management platforms, and business systems to provide actionable insights where decisions are made.

User acceptance requires that AI systems provide value to end users while being easy to understand and use. AI recommendations must be explainable and actionable, and users must trust the system's recommendations.

Ethical considerations include ensuring that AI systems don't create bias or discrimination, that worker privacy is protected, and that AI systems enhance rather than replace human judgment in safety decision-making.

# Building Your Technology Skills

As construction safety becomes increasingly digital, safety professionals need to develop technology skills that complement traditional safety expertise. These skills will become increasingly important for career advancement and professional effectiveness.

### Digital Literacy
Basic digital literacy skills are becoming essential for safety professionals. This includes understanding how digital systems work, how to evaluate technology solutions, and how to use data effectively in decision-making.

Understanding data and analytics is particularly important as safety management becomes more data-driven. You don't need to become a data scientist, but you should understand how to interpret data, identify trends, and use data to support safety decisions.

Technology evaluation skills help you assess new technologies and determine their potential value for your organization. This includes understanding implementation requirements, cost-benefit analysis, and integration considerations.

System integration knowledge helps you understand how different technologies work together and how to maximize value through effective system integration. This knowledge is essential for developing comprehensive technology strategies.

### Staying Current with Technology Trends
The pace of technology change requires continuous learning and adaptation. Developing strategies for staying current with technology trends will be essential throughout your career.

Professional development should include technology-focused training, conferences, and certification programs. Many safety organizations now offer technology-specific education and certification programs.

Networking with technology professionals and other safety professionals who are implementing new technologies provides valuable insights into practical implementation challenges and benefits.

Industry publications, websites, and social media provide ongoing information about new technologies and implementation case studies. Developing a regular routine for consuming this information helps you stay current with emerging trends.

Vendor relationships with technology providers can provide early access to new technologies and implementation support. Building relationships with key technology vendors in the construction safety space can provide competitive advantages.

**Implementation Leadership**
As you advance in your career, you'll likely be asked to lead technology implementation projects. Developing project management and change leadership skills will be essential for successful technology implementations.
Change management skills are particularly important for technology implementations that require changes in work processes, organizational structure, or culture. Understanding how to manage resistance to change and build support for new technologies is essential.

Training and communication skills help ensure that technology implementations are successful and that users can effectively utilize new systems. Developing capabilities to design and deliver technology training will be valuable throughout your career.

Performance measurement skills help you demonstrate the

value of technology investments and identify opportunities for improvement. Understanding how to measure technology ROI and effectiveness will be important for justifying continued investment in safety technology.

## Future Outlook

The technological transformation of construction safety is accelerating, and the pace of change will likely continue to increase. Understanding where the industry is heading can help you prepare for future opportunities and challenges.

### Emerging Technologies

Several emerging technologies show promise for further transforming construction safety in the coming years. Staying aware of these technologies and their potential applications will help you prepare for future developments.

Drone technology is becoming increasingly sophisticated and affordable, creating new opportunities for safety monitoring, inspection, and emergency response. Autonomous drones may soon provide continuous safety monitoring of large construction sites.

Robotics technology may begin to take over dangerous construction tasks, removing workers from high-risk situations. Understanding how robotics affects safety management will become increasingly important.

Advanced materials and smart clothing may provide new capabilities for worker protection and monitoring. Self-healing materials, adaptive protection systems, and integrated monitoring capabilities may become standard features of construction PPE.

Blockchain technology may provide new capabilities for safety record keeping, certification verification, and supply chain safety management. Understanding how blockchain can enhance safety management may become important for senior safety professionals.

**Industry Transformation**
The construction industry is undergoing fundamental changes that will affect how safety is managed. Understanding these broader industry trends will help you adapt your career strategy accordingly.
Digital transformation is affecting all aspects of construction, not just safety. Understanding how digital technologies are changing project delivery, business models, and organizational structures will help you position yourself for success in the digital construction industry.

Workforce changes including aging workers, skill shortages, and changing expectations are driving increased interest in technology solutions that can enhance worker capabilities and improve working conditions.

Regulatory evolution is beginning to incorporate new technologies into safety regulations and standards. Understanding how regulations are adapting to new technologies will be important for compliance and competitive advantage.

Client expectations are increasingly including requirements for advanced safety technologies and data transparency. Understanding how to meet these expectations will be important for business success.

# Preparing for the Technology-

# Enabled Future

Success in the technology-enabled future of construction safety requires preparing now for the changes that are coming. This preparation involves developing both technical skills and strategic thinking capabilities.

## Skills Development

Focus on developing skills that complement rather than compete with technology. While technology can automate many routine tasks, human skills such as critical thinking, problem-solving, communication, and leadership become more valuable.

Continuous learning capabilities will be essential as technology continues to evolve rapidly. Developing strategies for efficiently acquiring new knowledge and skills will be crucial for long-term career success.

Systems thinking skills become more important as safety systems become more complex and interconnected. Understanding how different technologies, processes, and organizational factors interact will be essential for effective safety management.

## Strategic Positioning

Position yourself as a bridge between traditional safety knowledge and emerging technologies. Organizations need safety professionals who can translate between technical safety requirements and technology capabilities.

Develop expertise in specific technology areas that align with your interests and career goals. Becoming known as an expert in particular technologies or applications can create unique career opportunities.

Build relationships with technology providers, other safety professionals who are implementing new technologies, and organizational leaders who are driving digital transformation initiatives.

Stay connected with broader industry trends beyond just safety technology. Understanding how construction industry transformation affects safety management will help you anticipate future changes and opportunities.

The future of construction safety is being shaped by technological innovation, and safety professionals who embrace these changes will have significant advantages in their careers. By developing technology skills, staying current with emerging trends, and positioning yourself as a technology-enabled safety leader, you can contribute to the industry's transformation while advancing your own career objectives.

In our next chapter, we'll explore how to build your professional network in this rapidly evolving industry, including how to connect with other technology-forward safety professionals and leverage professional relationships to advance your career and contribute to industry progress.

# CHAPTER 15: BUILDING YOUR PROFESSIONAL NETWORK

Your professional network will be one of your most valuable career assets as a construction safety professional. In an industry where relationships matter enormously, where knowledge sharing can literally save lives, and where career opportunities often come through personal connections, building and maintaining a strong professional network isn't just beneficial - it's essential for long-term success.

The construction safety community is surprisingly interconnected. Safety professionals regularly move between companies, share experiences across project sites, and collaborate on industry-wide safety initiatives. The relationships you build early in your career will continue to provide value throughout your professional journey, opening doors to new opportunities, providing access to critical knowledge, and offering support during challenging times.

Networking in construction safety goes beyond simple career advancement. When safety professionals share knowledge, best practices, and lessons learned, the entire industry benefits through improved safety performance and reduced injuries and fatalities. Your network becomes a channel for contributing to industry-wide safety improvements while advancing your own career objectives.

Understanding how to build, maintain, and leverage professional relationships will accelerate your career development and increase your effectiveness as a safety professional. This chapter will provide you with practical strategies for developing a robust professional network that supports both your career goals and your contribution to construction safety excellence.

## Professional Organizations and Associations

Professional organizations form the backbone of the construction safety community, providing structured opportunities for networking, learning, and professional development. Active participation in these organizations is one of the most effective ways to build your professional network while staying current with industry trends and best practices.

### Major Safety Organizations

The American Society of Safety Professionals (ASSP) is the premier organization for safety professionals across all industries, with strong representation in construction safety. ASSP offers local chapter meetings, national conferences, professional development programs, and networking opportunities that connect you with safety professionals at all career levels.

Local ASSP chapters provide regular meetings where you can meet other safety professionals in your area, learn about current issues and trends, and participate in professional development activities. These chapter meetings are particularly valuable for new safety professionals because they provide accessible networking opportunities and mentorship connections.

The National Safety Council (NSC) focuses on eliminating preventable deaths and injuries, with significant emphasis on workplace safety including construction. NSC provides networking opportunities through conferences, training programs, and special interest groups that connect safety professionals working on similar challenges.

The Board of Certified Safety Professionals (BCSP) administers professional certifications including the Certified Safety Professional (CSP) and Associate Safety Professional (ASP) credentials. While primarily a certification body, BCSP events and certification study groups provide valuable networking opportunities with other professionals pursuing similar credentials.

Industry-specific organizations such as the Associated General Contractors (AGC), the Construction Industry Safety Coalition (CISC), and regional construction associations often have safety committees or groups that provide networking opportunities focused specifically on construction safety challenges.

**Construction-Specific Organizations**
The Construction Industry Safety Coalition brings together safety professionals from major construction companies to

share best practices and collaborate on industry-wide safety initiatives. Participation in CISC activities provides access to cutting-edge safety practices and relationships with safety leaders from top-tier construction companies.

Regional construction safety organizations exist in many metropolitan areas, providing local networking opportunities and addressing region-specific safety challenges. These organizations often have lower barriers to entry and provide excellent opportunities for new professionals to get involved and build relationships.

Specialty trade organizations such as the International Association of Electrical Inspectors (IAEI), the Scaffold and Access Industry Association (SAIA), and the International Powered Access Federation (IPAF) provide networking opportunities for safety professionals focusing on specific trades or hazards.

Owner organizations such as the Construction Owners Association of America (COAA) and the Construction Users Roundtable (CURT) provide opportunities to network with client-side safety professionals and understand owner expectations for safety performance.

**Getting Involved Effectively**
Simply joining professional organizations isn't sufficient - you need to actively participate to build meaningful relationships and gain maximum value from your membership. Start by attending local meetings regularly and introducing yourself to other attendees. Don't wait for others to approach you; take initiative in meeting new people and learning about their experiences and challenges.

Volunteer for committee work or event planning activities.

These volunteer roles provide opportunities to work closely with other professionals while contributing to the organization's mission. Committee work often leads to lasting professional relationships and demonstrates your commitment to the profession.

Consider presenting at meetings or conferences about your experiences, projects, or lessons learned. Presenting positions you as a knowledge contributor and provides natural opportunities for others to approach you for further discussion. Even as a new professional, you can share fresh perspectives or innovative approaches that experienced professionals find valuable.

Attend social events and informal gatherings associated with meetings and conferences. Many of the most valuable networking connections happen during coffee breaks, lunch conversations, and after-hours social events where people can connect on a more personal level.

## Conference Attendance and Speaking Opportunities

Industry conferences provide concentrated networking opportunities where you can meet dozens of professionals in a few days while learning about the latest trends, technologies, and best practices. Strategic conference attendance can significantly accelerate your professional network development and career advancement.

### Major Industry Conferences

The American Society of Safety Professionals (ASSP) Professional Development Conference is the largest annual gathering of safety professionals in North America. This conference provides unparalleled networking opportunities through technical sessions, exhibit halls, social events, and structured networking activities.

The National Safety Council Congress & Expo combines safety education with extensive networking opportunities. The event attracts safety professionals from all industries, providing opportunities to learn from professionals in other sectors while building relationships within construction safety.

Construction-specific conferences such as the AGC Safety Conference, regional construction safety conferences, and specialty conferences focusing on specific hazards or technologies provide more targeted networking opportunities with professionals facing similar challenges.
International conferences such as the World Congress on Safety and Health at Work provide opportunities to build global networks and learn about international best practices that can be applied to domestic construction projects.

Technology-focused conferences are becoming increasingly important as construction safety becomes more digital. Events focusing on construction technology, safety technology, and digital transformation provide opportunities to network with technology-forward safety professionals and industry innovators.

**Maximizing Conference Value**
Prepare for conferences by reviewing the agenda, identifying speakers and attendees you want to meet, and setting specific networking goals. Many conferences provide attendee lists or mobile applications that help you identify and connect with other participants before and during the event.

Attend a mix of technical sessions, panel discussions,

and networking events to maximize your learning and relationship-building opportunities. Don't spend all your time in sessions - some of the most valuable conversations happen in exhibit halls, during breaks, and at social events.

Bring plenty of business cards and prepare a brief introduction that explains who you are, what you do, and what types of connections you're seeking. Practice your introduction so you can deliver it naturally and confidently when meeting new people.

Follow up promptly with new connections after the conference. Send personalized LinkedIn invitations or emails within a week of the conference, referencing your conversation and suggesting ways to stay in touch or collaborate.

Take notes about the people you meet, including their contact information, companies, areas of expertise, and personal details that can help you maintain relationships over time. These notes are invaluable for follow-up conversations and future interactions.

**Speaking and Presenting**
Speaking at conferences and industry events significantly enhances your professional visibility and networking opportunities. When you present, other attendees approach you to discuss your topic, share their experiences, and explore potential collaboration opportunities.

Start with local chapter meetings or regional conferences where the audience is smaller and less intimidating. These speaking opportunities help you develop presentation skills while building relationships with local professionals.

Propose presentations based on your actual experiences, projects, or research rather than theoretical topics. Real-world case studies and lessons learned presentations tend to generate more audience interest and networking opportunities.

Panel discussions and roundtable formats provide excellent speaking opportunities for newer professionals. These formats allow you to contribute your perspective while learning from more experienced panelists.
Consider co-presenting with colleagues or industry partners. Co-presentations can reduce individual preparation burden while expanding your networking reach through your co-presenter's professional network.

**Building Speaking Expertise**
Develop expertise in specific areas that align with your career interests and market demand. Becoming known as an expert in emerging technologies, specific hazards, or innovative safety approaches creates speaking opportunities and positions you as a thought leader.

Practice your presentation skills through local organizations, company meetings, and low-stakes speaking opportunities. Good presentation skills make you a more attractive speaker for major conferences and more effective in networking situations.

Create compelling presentation materials that clearly communicate your key messages and provide value to audience members. High-quality presentations enhance your professional reputation and make conference organizers more likely to invite you back.

Collect testimonials and feedback from your presentations to improve your skills and provide evidence of your speaking effectiveness to future conference organizers.

## Social Media and Online Presence

Digital networking through social media and online platforms has become increasingly important for professional relationship building. These platforms allow you to connect with professionals worldwide, share knowledge, and build your professional brand beyond geographical limitations.

### LinkedIn for Safety Professionals

LinkedIn is the most important professional social media platform for construction safety professionals. A well-crafted LinkedIn profile serves as your digital business card and provides opportunities to connect with professionals you might never meet in person.

Optimize your LinkedIn profile with a professional photo, compelling headline, and detailed summary that clearly communicates your expertise and career interests. Use industry keywords that help other professionals find you when searching for specific expertise.

Share relevant content regularly, including industry articles, project updates, lessons learned, and insights about safety trends. Consistent content sharing establishes you as an active member of the professional community and provides opportunities for engagement with your network.

Engage with other professionals' content by commenting thoughtfully on posts, sharing relevant articles, and participating in professional discussions. This engagement increases your visibility and demonstrates your expertise to a broader audience.

Join LinkedIn groups focused on construction safety, specific hazards, or geographic regions. These groups provide opportunities to participate in professional discussions, share knowledge, and connect with professionals who share similar interests.

Use LinkedIn's advanced search features to identify and connect with professionals at specific companies, with particular expertise, or in specific geographic areas. Personalize connection requests with brief messages explaining why you want to connect.

**Professional Blogging and Content Creation**
Creating original content through blogging, articles, or social media posts establishes you as a thought leader and provides natural opportunities for other professionals to connect with you. Content creation doesn't require being a professional writer - focus on sharing practical insights and experiences that provide value to other safety professionals.

Write about your actual experiences, projects, and lessons learned rather than theoretical topics. Real-world content tends to generate more engagement and provides more networking value than abstract discussions.

Share content across multiple platforms including LinkedIn, company websites, industry publications, and professional organization newsletters. Multi-platform sharing maximizes your content's reach and networking potential.

Engage with comments and feedback on your content. Responding to comments and questions provides opportunities to deepen relationships with readers and demonstrate your expertise.

Consider guest posting for industry publications, professional organization newsletters, or other professionals' blogs. Guest posting expands your reach beyond your immediate network while providing valuable content to other platforms.

**Twitter (X) and Other Platforms**
Twitter (X) provides opportunities for real-time engagement with industry conversations and quick connections with other professionals. While less formal than LinkedIn, Twitter (X) can be valuable for staying current with industry trends and participating in professional discussions.

Follow industry leaders, safety organizations, and news sources to stay current with industry developments. Engage with their content through likes, retweets, and thoughtful comments to build relationships and increase your visibility.

Use relevant hashtags to increase the visibility of your tweets and connect with conversations about specific topics. Common construction safety hashtags include #ConstructionSafety, #SafetyFirst, #SafetyProfessional, and #SafetyLeadership.

Share quick insights, industry news, and behind-the-scenes content that provides value to your followers while showcasing your expertise and personality.

YouTube and other video platforms provide opportunities to create more engaging content while demonstrating your communication skills and expertise. Video content often generates higher engagement rates than text-based content.

**Online Reputation Management**
Your online presence becomes part of your professional

reputation, so it's important to maintain a consistent, professional image across all platforms. Regularly review your social media profiles and content to ensure they align with your professional goals.

Be authentic in your online interactions while maintaining professionalism. People connect with real personalities, but remember that your online presence represents your professional brand.

Monitor your online reputation by regularly searching for your name and professional information. Address any negative content or misinformation promptly and professionally.

Consider creating a simple personal website that showcases your expertise, experience, and professional accomplishments. A professional website serves as a central hub for your online presence and provides a platform for sharing detailed information about your background and capabilities.

## Mentoring Others as You Advance

As you progress in your career, mentoring others becomes both a professional responsibility and a powerful networking strategy. Mentoring relationships create lasting professional bonds while contributing to industry development and your own leadership skills.

### Benefits of Mentoring

Mentoring others reinforces your own knowledge and skills while helping you stay current with emerging trends and fresh perspectives. New professionals often bring innovative ideas and approaches that can enhance your own professional effectiveness.

Mentoring relationships often evolve into lasting professional relationships that provide mutual benefit throughout both parties' careers. Many successful safety professionals maintain relationships with their mentors and mentees for decades.

Mentoring demonstrates leadership capabilities and professional maturity that are valued by employers and clients. Organizations increasingly recognize mentoring contributions when making promotion and advancement decisions.

Contributing to others' professional development provides personal satisfaction and reinforces your commitment to the safety profession. Many experienced professionals find mentoring to be one of the most rewarding aspects of their careers.

**Finding Mentoring Opportunities**
Formal mentoring programs offered by professional organizations, companies, and educational institutions provide structured mentoring opportunities with clear expectations and support resources.

Informal mentoring relationships often develop naturally through professional interactions, volunteer work, and conference connections. These relationships may be less structured but can be equally valuable for both mentors and mentees.

Reverse mentoring, where experienced professionals learn from newer professionals about emerging technologies, generational perspectives, or fresh approaches, provides mutual benefit and creates strong professional bonds.

Group mentoring, where experienced professionals work with small groups of newer professionals, provides efficient ways to share knowledge while building multiple professional relationships simultaneously.

**Effective Mentoring Practices**
Set clear expectations and boundaries for mentoring relationships, including communication frequency, meeting formats, and specific goals or objectives. Clear expectations help ensure that both parties gain maximum value from the relationship.

Focus on sharing practical knowledge, real-world experiences, and career insights rather than theoretical information that mentees can find elsewhere. Your unique experiences and perspectives provide the most value to mentees.

Encourage mentees to take ownership of their professional development while providing guidance and support. Effective mentoring empowers mentees to make their own decisions rather than simply following directions.

Connect mentees with your broader professional network when appropriate. Introducing mentees to other professionals expands their networking opportunities while strengthening your own relationships.
Maintain appropriate boundaries between mentoring and personal relationships. While mentoring relationships can become personally meaningful, it's important to maintain professional focus and boundaries.

**Building Mentoring Networks**

Consider participating in multiple mentoring relationships simultaneously, both as a mentor and as a mentee. Even experienced professionals can benefit from mentoring relationships with other professionals who have different expertise or perspectives.

Create informal mentoring networks by connecting professionals at different career stages who can learn from each other. These networks can be particularly effective for addressing specific challenges or developing expertise in particular areas.

Leverage technology to maintain mentoring relationships across geographic distances. Video conferencing, email, and social media platforms make it possible to maintain meaningful mentoring relationships without regular in-person meetings.

Document lessons learned from your mentoring experiences and share them with other professionals who are considering mentoring relationships. Your insights can help others develop effective mentoring practices.

# Leveraging Your Network for Career Growth

Building a professional network is only valuable if you know how to leverage it effectively for career advancement, knowledge sharing, and professional opportunities. Understanding how to activate your network appropriately while maintaining authentic relationships is crucial for long-term success.

### Job Search and Career Opportunities

Many of the best career opportunities are never publicly

advertised - they're filled through professional networks before companies invest in formal recruiting processes. Your network can provide early access to these hidden opportunities while offering insights into company culture and position requirements.

Inform your network about your career interests and goals without appearing desperate or overly aggressive. Share your career objectives during natural conversations and through professional updates on social media platforms.

Ask for informational interviews with professionals in companies or roles that interest you. These conversations provide valuable insights into career paths and company cultures while maintaining relationships that might lead to future opportunities.

Request introductions to professionals at companies where you're interested in working. Your network contacts can provide valuable introductions that help you stand out from other candidates while giving you insider perspectives on opportunities.

Consider your network contacts as references who can speak to your professional capabilities and character. Maintain these relationships proactively so that contacts are prepared to provide strong recommendations when needed.

## Knowledge Sharing and Problem Solving

Your professional network serves as a distributed knowledge base where you can find expertise, solutions, and perspectives on virtually any safety challenge you encounter. Learning to tap into this knowledge effectively can significantly enhance your professional effectiveness.

Reach out to network contacts when facing unfamiliar challenges or seeking best practices for specific situations.

Most safety professionals are willing to share their experiences and insights when asked appropriately.

Participate in professional forums, discussion groups, and online communities where safety professionals share knowledge and solve problems collaboratively. These platforms provide access to collective wisdom while building new professional relationships.

Offer your own expertise and assistance to others in your network when you have relevant knowledge or experience. Providing value to others strengthens relationships and creates reciprocal obligations that benefit you in the future.

Consider forming or joining professional study groups or mastermind groups where small numbers of professionals meet regularly to share challenges, solutions, and accountability for professional development goals.

**Business Development and Partnerships**
As you advance in your career, your professional network becomes increasingly important for business development, whether you're working for a company that needs to win new clients or considering consulting or independent practice.

Your network provides referral sources for new business opportunities and partnerships. Satisfied clients and professional contacts often recommend safety professionals they know and trust to others who need similar services.

Collaborate with other professionals on projects, proposals, and business development initiatives. These collaborations can lead to new opportunities while strengthening professional relationships.

Consider your network when seeking strategic partnerships

or joint venture opportunities. Your professional relationships can provide the foundation for business partnerships that create mutual value.

Maintain relationships with former colleagues and clients who might become future business partners or referral sources. These relationships often provide the most valuable business development opportunities.

## Maintaining Network Relationships

Professional networks require ongoing maintenance to remain valuable. Relationships that aren't nurtured tend to weaken over time, reducing their value for all parties involved.

Stay in regular contact with key network contacts through periodic emails, social media interactions, and in-person meetings when possible. The frequency of contact should match the strength and importance of the relationship.

Provide value to your network contacts through relevant information sharing, introductions to other professionals, and assistance with their professional challenges. Relationships that provide mutual value tend to be stronger and more durable.

Remember personal details about your network contacts and acknowledge important events such as promotions, job changes, and professional achievements. These personal touches strengthen relationships and demonstrate that you value the connection.

Be patient and authentic in your networking efforts. Genuine relationships take time to develop and provide the most value over the long term. Avoid transactional approaches that focus solely on immediate benefits.

# Global Networking and International Connections

The construction industry is increasingly global, with companies working on international projects and safety professionals moving between countries throughout their careers. Building international connections provides access to global best practices while creating opportunities for international career advancement.

### International Professional Organizations

Many professional organizations have international chapters or affiliations that provide opportunities to connect with safety professionals worldwide. The International Association for the Study of Pain (IASP), the International Labour Organization (ILO), and regional organizations provide global networking opportunities.

International conferences and events provide concentrated opportunities to build global professional relationships while learning about international best practices and regulatory approaches.

Consider participating in international professional exchanges, study tours, or collaborative projects that provide opportunities to work directly with international colleagues while building lasting relationships.
Online platforms and social media make it easier than ever to maintain international professional relationships and stay current with global industry developments.

### Cultural Considerations

Building international professional relationships requires sensitivity to cultural differences in communication styles, business practices, and relationship-building approaches. What works in one culture may not be effective in another.

Invest time in understanding the business cultures and communication preferences of international colleagues. This cultural competence enhances your effectiveness in international networking and business relationships.

Be patient with international relationship building, as many cultures prefer to develop trust gradually through multiple interactions rather than immediate business-focused relationships.

Consider language barriers and communication preferences when building international relationships. Some professionals may prefer written communication while others prefer verbal interactions.

**Leveraging International Connections**
International connections can provide access to global job opportunities, international project assignments, and exposure to innovative safety practices developed in other countries.

Consider how international best practices might be adapted for use in domestic projects while respecting local regulations and cultural preferences.

International relationships can provide valuable perspectives on global industry trends and emerging challenges that may eventually affect domestic markets.

Building international expertise and relationships can differentiate you from other safety professionals while creating unique career opportunities in global construction companies.

## Your Networking Action Plan

Successful networking requires intentional effort and strategic planning. Developing a personal networking action plan helps ensure that your networking activities align with your career goals while making efficient use of your time and energy.

### Setting Networking Goals

Define specific networking objectives that align with your career goals, such as meeting a certain number of new professionals each quarter, joining specific professional organizations, or attending particular conferences.

Identify the types of professionals you want to connect with, such as safety managers at specific companies, experts in particular hazards, or professionals in specific geographic regions.

Set measurable goals for your networking activities, such as the number of new LinkedIn connections per month, the frequency of professional organization meeting attendance, or the number of informational interviews you conduct.

Regularly review and adjust your networking goals based on your evolving career objectives and the effectiveness of your networking activities.

### Tracking Your Network

Maintain a systematic approach to tracking your professional relationships, including contact information, interaction history, and relevant personal and professional details.
Use customer relationship management (CRM) tools,

spreadsheets, or dedicated networking applications to organize your professional contacts and track relationship maintenance activities.

Set reminders for regular contact with key network relationships and track the frequency and quality of your interactions with different professionals.

Document the value you've received from your professional network and the value you've provided to others. This documentation helps you understand the return on your networking investment and identify areas for improvement.

**Continuous Improvement**
Regularly assess the effectiveness of your networking activities and adjust your approach based on what's working well and what needs improvement.

Seek feedback from trusted network contacts about your networking effectiveness and areas where you might improve your relationship-building skills.

Experiment with different networking approaches and platforms to find what works best for your personality, schedule, and career objectives.

Invest in developing your relationship-building skills through training, reading, and practice. Strong networking skills provide career-long benefits that justify the investment in skill development.

Building a strong professional network is one of the most important investments you can make in your construction safety career. The relationships you build will provide knowledge, opportunities, and support throughout your professional journey while allowing you to contribute to industry-wide safety improvements. By approaching networking strategically and authentically, you can build a network that serves both your career objectives and your commitment to construction safety excellence.

In our next chapter, we'll explore specific career advancement strategies that leverage your growing expertise, professional network, and industry knowledge to accelerate your progress toward senior safety leadership roles.

# CHAPTER 16: CAREER ADVANCEMENT STRATEGIES

After establishing yourself as a competent safety professional, the question becomes: where do you go from here? Career advancement in construction safety isn't just about climbing a traditional corporate ladder - it's about expanding your influence, deepening your expertise, and creating more significant impact on worker safety across the industry.

This chapter will guide you through the various pathways for advancing your safety career, from specialized technical roles to executive leadership positions, and everything in between.

## Understanding Career Progression in Construction Safety

Construction safety careers typically follow several distinct pathways, each offering unique opportunities for growth and impact. Unlike many professions with linear advancement structures, safety careers often involve lateral moves that build breadth of experience before vertical advancement.

**Traditional Progression Path:**
- Safety Technician/Specialist → Senior Safety Specialist → Safety Manager → Safety Director → VP of Safety/Risk Management

**Alternative Pathways:**
- Consulting and independent practice
- Training and education specialization
- Regulatory and compliance roles
- Technology and innovation positions
- Research and development opportunities

The key to successful advancement lies in understanding that each role requires different skill sets and offers different rewards. A safety director needs strong business acumen and leadership skills, while a specialist consultant might focus on deep technical expertise in specific hazard areas.

# Specialization Areas Within Construction Safety

As the construction industry becomes more complex and specialized, so do the opportunities for safety professionals. Developing expertise in specific areas can significantly accelerate your career advancement and increase your market value.

### High-Demand Specialization Areas

**Industrial Construction Safety** Petrochemical, power generation, and manufacturing facilities present unique challenges requiring specialized knowledge of process safety management, hazardous materials handling, and complex regulatory compliance. Professionals in this area often command premium salaries due to the critical nature of the work and specialized skill requirements.

**Infrastructure and Heavy Civil** Bridge construction, tunneling, highway projects, and major civil works require expertise in heavy equipment operations, traffic control, and coordination with multiple agencies. This specialization offers opportunities to work on landmark projects that shape communities for generations.

**High-Rise and Complex Building Construction** Skyscrapers, hospitals, and other complex structures present unique fall protection challenges, coordination complexities, and sophisticated safety system requirements. Specialists in this area often work in major metropolitan markets with corresponding salary premiums.

**Environmental Health and Safety Integration** As sustainability becomes more important, professionals who can integrate environmental compliance with traditional safety management are increasingly valuable. This specialization often leads to broader EHS management roles.

**Technology and Digital Safety** The integration of drones, sensors, wearable technology, and data analytics in construction safety creates opportunities for tech-savvy professionals to bridge the gap between traditional safety practice and emerging technologies.

## Developing Your Specialization

Choose your specialization based on a combination of market demand, personal interest, and natural aptitudes. Consider:
- **Geographic factors**: What types of construction are prominent in your region?
- **Industry trends**: Which sectors are growing and investing in safety?
- **Personal strengths**: Do you excel at technical analysis, relationship building, or strategic thinking?
- **Market compensation**: Research salary ranges and growth potential in different specializations

Once you've identified your target specialization, invest in relevant training, certifications, and project experience. Seek out mentors already working in your chosen area and consider taking temporary assignments or consulting projects to build credibility.

# Transitioning to Consulting and Management Roles

Many experienced safety professionals eventually consider independent consulting or transitioning to senior management positions. Both paths offer increased autonomy and earning potential but require different preparation strategies.

### Building a Successful Safety Consulting Practice
**Advantages of Consulting:**
- Higher earning potential
- Flexibility and autonomy
- Exposure to diverse projects and challenges
- Opportunity to specialize deeply
- Geographic freedom

**Prerequisites for Success:**
- Established reputation and network
- Deep expertise in specific areas
- Strong business development skills
- Financial management capabilities
- Risk tolerance for irregular income

**Steps to Transition:**
1. **Build your reputation while employed**: Speak at conferences, write articles, and become known for specific expertise
2. **Develop a financial cushion**: Save 6-12 months of expenses to weather initial income variability
3. **Start part-time**: Take on small projects evenings and

weekends to test the waters
4. **Create professional infrastructure**: Establish business entity, insurance, contracts, and marketing materials
5. **Develop a pipeline**: Build relationships with potential clients before making the leap

## Advancing to Senior Management

Safety directors and VPs of Safety/Risk Management play strategic roles in organizational success, requiring skills beyond traditional safety expertise.

**Key Management Competencies:**
- **Financial acumen**: Understanding budgets, ROI calculations, and cost-benefit analysis
- **Strategic thinking**: Aligning safety initiatives with business objectives
- **Leadership**: Inspiring and developing teams across multiple projects or facilities
- **Stakeholder management**: Working effectively with executives, union representatives, and external partners
- **Change management**: Leading organizational transformation initiatives

**Preparation Strategies:**
- Pursue an MBA or executive education programs
- Seek cross-functional assignments in operations, HR, or project management
- Lead major initiatives that demonstrate business impact
- Develop presentation and communication skills for board-level audiences
- Build relationships with senior leaders across the organization

# Salary Negotiation and Career Mobility

Understanding your market value and negotiating effectively are crucial skills for career advancement. The construction safety profession offers significant earning potential, but maximizing your compensation requires strategic thinking and negotiation skills.

## Understanding Market Compensation
### Factors Affecting Salary:
- Geographic location and cost of living
- Industry sector and project complexity
- Company size and safety culture maturity
- Individual certifications and education
- Years of experience and track record
- Specialized skills and expertise areas

### Research Resources:
- Professional association salary surveys
- Online compensation databases (Glassdoor, PayScale, Salary.com)
- Networking with peers in similar roles
- Executive recruiters specializing in safety positions
- Industry publications and reports

## Negotiation Strategies
### Prepare Thoroughly:
- Document your accomplishments with specific metrics
- Research comparable positions and salary ranges
- Understand the complete compensation package, not just base salary
- Consider timing - annual reviews, successful project completions, or new certifications

**Negotiation Tactics:**
- Focus on value delivered rather than personal needs
- Use industry benchmarks and data to support requests
- Consider non-salary benefits: professional development, flexible work arrangements, additional responsibilities
- Be prepared to discuss career advancement timelines and opportunities

**Beyond Base Salary:**
- Performance bonuses tied to safety metrics
- Professional development funding
- Conference attendance and speaking opportunities
- Equipment and technology budgets
- Flexible work arrangements
- Additional vacation time
- Professional membership reimbursements

## Strategic Career Mobility

**Internal Advancement:**
- Seek stretch assignments on high-visibility projects
- Volunteer for cross-functional teams and committees
- Mentor junior staff and build leadership reputation
- Document and communicate safety program ROI
- Build relationships across the organization

**External Opportunities:**
- Maintain professional network even when happily employed
- Keep resume updated with recent accomplishments
- Consider contract or temporary assignments for skill building
- Build reputation through professional activities and thought leadership
- Work with executive recruiters specializing in safety roles

# Work-Life Balance in Safety Careers

Construction safety professionals often work demanding schedules, especially during active construction phases. However, advancing your career doesn't have to come at the expense of personal well-being and family relationships.

## Managing Demanding Schedules
**Project-Based Challenges:**
- Long hours during critical construction phases
- Travel requirements for multi-site responsibilities
- Emergency response and incident investigation demands
- Pressure to be available during all work hours

**Strategies for Balance:**
- Set clear boundaries and communicate them consistently
- Use technology efficiently to maximize productivity
- Delegate effectively as you advance to management roles
- Plan personal time around project schedules when possible
- Negotiate flexible arrangements during less intensive periods

## Sustainable Career Practices
**Physical and Mental Health:**
- Regular exercise routines that accommodate irregular schedules
- Stress management techniques for high-pressure situations
- Professional counseling or coaching when needed
- Regular health checkups and preventive care
- Time for hobbies and personal interests

**Family and Relationship Considerations:**
- Include family in career planning discussions
- Create rituals and traditions that provide stability
- Use technology to stay connected during travel

- Plan family vacations during project downtime
- Consider geographic stability when evaluating opportunities

**Professional Development:**
- Integrate learning into daily work rather than adding to schedule
- Choose conferences and training that provide both professional value and personal enjoyment
- Find mentoring relationships that offer flexibility
- Use commute time for professional podcasts or audiobooks

## Long-Term Career Sustainability

As you advance in your safety career, consider how your choices today will affect your long-term satisfaction and effectiveness. Many senior safety professionals report that their most rewarding career phases came after they learned to balance professional achievement with personal fulfillment.

**Questions for Self-Reflection:**
- What aspects of safety work energize you most?
- How do you define success beyond salary and title?
- What legacy do you want to leave in the safety profession?
- How can you structure your career to remain passionate about the work?
- What role do you want work to play in your overall life satisfaction?

# Creating Your Advancement Action Plan

Successful career advancement rarely happens by accident. It requires intentional planning, consistent effort, and regular evaluation of progress toward your goals.

## Five-Year Career Planning

**Assessment Phase:**
1. Evaluate current position and satisfaction level
2. Identify target roles and required qualifications
3. Assess gaps in skills, experience, or credentials
4. Research market conditions and opportunities
5. Consider personal and family factors

**Development Phase:**
1. Create specific learning and development goals
2. Identify mentors and networking opportunities
3. Plan certification and education timeline
4. Seek stretch assignments and new responsibilities
5. Build visibility through professional activities

**Implementation Phase:**
1. Execute development plan consistently
2. Track progress and adjust as needed
3. Build and maintain professional network
4. Document accomplishments and build portfolio
5. Evaluate opportunities against career goals

## Annual Career Review Process
**Professional Accomplishments:**
- Safety performance improvements achieved
- Cost savings or ROI generated
- Team development and mentoring activities
- Innovation or process improvement initiatives
- Recognition and awards received

**Skill Development:**
- New certifications or credentials earned
- Training programs completed
- Conference presentations given
- Articles or thought leadership published
- Technical skills developed

**Network Expansion:**

- New professional relationships built
- Mentoring relationships established
- Industry committee or volunteer work
- Speaking opportunities accepted
- Community involvement activities

**Goal Adjustment:**
- Progress toward stated objectives
- Market changes affecting career path
- Personal priority shifts
- New opportunities discovered
- Skills or interests evolved

Remember that career advancement is not just about reaching the next level - it's about continuously growing your ability to protect workers and influence safety culture across the construction industry. The most successful safety professionals are those who remain passionate about the fundamental mission of preventing injuries and saving lives, even as they take on broader responsibilities and greater challenges.

Your career advancement should ultimately serve both your personal goals and the greater good of construction safety. When you succeed in advancing your career while maintaining this focus, you join the ranks of safety leaders who are transforming the construction industry for the better.

# CHAPTER 17: ETHICAL CONSIDERATIONS AND PROFESSIONAL RESPONSIBILITY

Construction safety professionals occupy a unique position of trust and responsibility. Workers depend on your expertise to return home safely each day, while employers rely on your judgment to protect their business and reputation. This dual responsibility creates complex ethical situations that require careful consideration and principled decision-making.

Unlike many professions where ethical dilemmas are theoretical exercises, safety professionals face real-world situations where the wrong decision can result in serious injury or death. The weight of this responsibility shapes every aspect of professional practice and demands the highest standards of ethical conduct.

# The Foundation of Safety Ethics

Safety ethics extend beyond simple rule-following or regulatory compliance. They encompass a comprehensive framework of moral principles that guide decision-making when facing competing interests, unclear situations, or pressure to compromise safety standards.

## Core Ethical Principles in Safety

**The Primacy of Human Life and Well-being** This fundamental principle establishes that protecting human life and preventing injury takes precedence over other considerations. When production schedules, cost concerns, or convenience conflict with worker safety, the ethical safety professional always prioritizes human well-being.

This doesn't mean safety considerations always override other factors, but rather that any decision potentially affecting worker safety must give appropriate weight to human consequences. The challenge lies in determining what constitutes "appropriate weight" in complex situations.

**Professional Competence and Continuous Learning** Safety professionals have an ethical obligation to maintain and expand their knowledge and skills. Accepting assignments beyond your competence, failing to stay current with evolving standards, or providing advice in areas where you lack expertise violates this fundamental principle.

This principle requires honest self-assessment and the humility to seek help when facing unfamiliar situations. It also demands investment in continuing education and professional development throughout your career.

**Honesty and Transparency** Safety professionals must provide accurate, complete information even when the truth is uncomfortable or inconvenient. This includes reporting safety violations, acknowledging mistakes, and presenting balanced assessments of risks and mitigation strategies.

Transparency extends to conflicts of interest, limitations in your knowledge or experience, and the assumptions underlying your recommendations. Workers and employers deserve complete information to make informed decisions about safety risks.

**Fairness and Respect for Persons** Every worker, regardless of position, background, or personal characteristics, deserves equal protection and consideration. Safety standards and enforcement must be applied consistently across all levels of the organization.

This principle challenges safety professionals to examine their own biases and ensure that safety programs serve all workers effectively, including those from different cultural backgrounds, languages, or experience levels.

## The Professional Duty of Care

As a safety professional, you assume a special duty of care that extends beyond typical employment relationships. This duty creates legal and ethical obligations that persist even when facing pressure to compromise standards.

**Elements of Professional Duty:**
- **Reasonable care**: Applying the knowledge, skill, and judgment expected of competent safety professionals
- **Loyalty**: Acting in the best interests of worker safety while fulfilling employer obligations
- **Confidentiality**: Protecting sensitive information while ensuring appropriate safety communications
- **Independence**: Maintaining professional judgment despite external pressures

Understanding this duty helps clarify your role when facing competing demands from different stakeholders.

## Common Ethical Dilemmas in Safety Practice

Real-world safety practice presents numerous situations where ethical principles conflict with practical pressures. Understanding common dilemma patterns helps prepare you for principled decision-making when these situations arise.

### Production Pressure vs. Safety Requirements

Perhaps the most frequent ethical challenge involves balancing production demands with safety requirements. These situations typically arise when:
- Schedule pressures tempt shortcuts around safety procedures
- Cost constraints limit resources for adequate safety measures
- Management questions the necessity of safety requirements
- Workers resist safety measures that slow their work

**Case Example**: A project superintendent approaches you three days before a critical deadline, explaining that the required fall protection setup will delay concrete placement by eight hours. He suggests that experienced workers can safely perform the work without full protection "just this once." Missing the deadline will result in significant financial penalties for the company.

**Ethical Analysis Framework**:
1. **Identify stakeholders**: Workers at risk, company financial interests, project team, families of workers
2. **Assess consequences**: Potential for serious injury or death vs. financial penalty

3. **Apply ethical principles**: Does compromising safety violate your fundamental duty to protect workers?
4. **Consider alternatives**: Are there creative solutions that address both safety and schedule concerns?
5. **Make principled decision**: Choose the option that best upholds your ethical obligations

**Resolution Approach**: Work with the project team to identify alternative methods, accelerated fall protection setup procedures, or schedule modifications that protect workers while minimizing project impact. If no acceptable alternatives exist, safety must take precedence.

## Conflicting Regulations and Standards

Construction projects often involve multiple regulatory jurisdictions, industry standards, and client requirements that may conflict with each other. Safety professionals must navigate these conflicts while maintaining ethical standards.

**Common Scenarios:**
- OSHA standards differ from more stringent client requirements
- Local regulations conflict with industry best practices
- International projects involve different safety standards
- Union agreements include safety provisions that differ from company policies

**Ethical Approach**: When standards conflict, apply the most protective requirements unless doing so creates greater overall risk. Document your decision-making process and communicate clearly with all stakeholders about which standards you're applying and why.

## Information Disclosure and Confidentiality

Safety professionals often possess sensitive information about workplace hazards, incident investigations, or regulatory violations. Determining when and how to share this information presents ethical challenges.

**Balancing Considerations:**
- Worker right to know about hazards
- Company concerns about competitive information
- Legal requirements for disclosure
- Potential for information misuse

**Guidelines for Ethical Information Handling:**
- Err on the side of disclosure when worker safety is at stake
- Distinguish between truly confidential business information and safety-related data
- Clearly communicate the basis for your disclosure decisions
- Seek legal counsel when facing unclear disclosure requirements

## Personal Relationships and Professional Judgment

Construction is often a relationship-based industry where personal connections influence business decisions. Safety professionals must maintain objectivity despite personal relationships with colleagues, supervisors, or contractors.

**Potential Conflicts:**
- Friends or family members working for contractors you must evaluate
- Social relationships with management who make safety-related decisions
- Financial interests in companies affected by your safety recommendations
- Personal career concerns influencing safety decisions

**Maintaining Professional Integrity:**
- Disclose potential conflicts of interest proactively

- Recuse yourself from decisions where conflicts cannot be managed
- Apply safety standards consistently regardless of personal relationships
- Separate personal and professional considerations in decision-making

# Whistleblower Protections and Responsibilities

Safety professionals have both legal protections and ethical obligations when witnessing serious safety violations or retaliation against workers who raise safety concerns.

### Legal Framework for Whistleblower Protection

**OSHA Whistleblower Protection Program** covers employees who report:
- Work-related injuries or illnesses
- Unsafe or unhealthful working conditions
- Violations of various safety and environmental statutes
- Retaliation for participating in OSHA inspections or proceedings

**Protection Scope**: Federal law prohibits employers from retaliating against employees who exercise their rights under workplace safety laws. Retaliation can include firing, demotion, harassment, or other adverse employment actions.

**Time Limits**: Most whistleblower complaints must be filed within 30 days of the alleged retaliation, though some statutes allow longer periods.

## Professional Obligations in Whistleblowing Situations

**When You Witness Violations**: Safety professionals have an ethical duty to report serious safety violations through appropriate channels, even when doing so may create personal or professional consequences.

**When Others Report to You**: Create safe reporting mechanisms and respond promptly to safety concerns raised by workers. Never ignore or discourage legitimate safety reports.

**When You Experience Retaliation**: Document incidents carefully and seek appropriate legal counsel. Your willingness to stand up for safety principles protects not only your own integrity but also the broader profession.

## Best Practices for Ethical Reporting

**Internal Reporting First**: Generally, attempt to resolve safety concerns through internal channels before involving external agencies, unless immediate danger exists or internal processes have proven ineffective.

**Documentation**: Maintain detailed records of safety concerns, communications, and responses. This documentation protects both workers and your professional reputation.

**Professional Networks**: Connect with other safety professionals who can provide guidance and support when facing difficult reporting decisions.

**Legal Resources**: Understand your rights and available legal protections before you need them. Professional associations often provide legal resources for members facing ethical dilemmas.

# Professional Codes of Conduct

Professional safety organizations establish codes of conduct that provide specific guidance for ethical decision-making. Understanding and following these codes demonstrates your commitment to professional standards.

## American Society of Safety Professionals (ASSP) Code of Ethics

**Key Principles:**
- Hold paramount the safety, health, and welfare of the public
- Perform services only in areas of competence
- Issue public statements only in an objective and truthful manner
- Act in professional matters as faithful agents of employers while prioritizing public safety
- Avoid conflicts of interest and disclose unavoidable conflicts
- Build professional reputation on merit and refrain from unfair competition

**Practical Application**: These principles provide a framework for decision-making when facing ethical dilemmas. When uncertain about the right course of action, consider which choice best upholds these fundamental commitments.

## Board of Certified Safety Professionals (BCSP) Code of Ethics

**Core Elements:**
- Protect the safety, health, and welfare of the public
- Practice only in areas of competence
- Maintain objectivity and integrity in professional services
- Avoid conflicts of interest
- Build professional reputation through honest practice
- Support professional development of safety

practitioners

**Certification Implications**: Certified safety professionals who violate ethical standards may face disciplinary action, including suspension or revocation of certification credentials.

**Industry-Specific Codes**
Many construction industry organizations have established their own ethical standards:

**Associated General Contractors (AGC)** emphasizes safety leadership and worker protection in construction operations.
**Construction Industry Institute (CII)** promotes research-based practices that include ethical considerations in safety management.

**International Association of Fire Chiefs (IAFC)** provides guidance for safety professionals working in emergency response and fire protection.
Understanding the ethical standards relevant to your specific work environment helps ensure comprehensive ethical practice.

# Balancing Production Pressures with Safety Requirements
The fundamental tension between production efficiency and safety requirements creates ongoing ethical challenges for construction safety professionals. Successfully managing this balance requires understanding both the legitimate business concerns and the non-negotiable safety principles.

## Understanding Production Pressures
**Legitimate Business Concerns:**

- Project schedules with contractual penalties for delays
- Cost control in competitive bidding environments
- Weather windows for critical construction activities
- Coordination with multiple trades and subcontractors
- Client expectations and long-term business relationships

**Recognizing Inappropriate Pressure:**
- Requests to ignore or circumvent safety regulations
- Suggestions that safety requirements are unnecessary or excessive
- Pressure to approve unsafe work practices to save time or money
- Attempts to blame safety requirements for project problems
- Retaliation threats for maintaining safety standards

## Ethical Decision-Making Framework
### Step 1: Clarify the Situation
- What specific safety requirements are being questioned?
- What are the stated reasons for seeking alternatives?
- Who are the affected stakeholders?
- What are the potential consequences of different choices?

### Step 2: Identify Creative Alternatives
- Can safety requirements be met through different methods?
- Are there ways to improve efficiency while maintaining safety?
- Would additional resources resolve the conflict?
- Can scheduling or sequencing changes address both concerns?

### Step 3: Communicate Value Proposition
- Explain the reasoning behind safety requirements
- Quantify potential consequences of compromising

safety
- Propose alternative solutions that address business concerns
- Document agreements and decisions clearly

**Step 4: Hold the Line When Necessary**
- Recognize when safety cannot be compromised
- Explain your professional and ethical obligations
- Escalate to appropriate management levels if needed
- Document your position and reasoning

## Building Credibility Through Consistency

**Demonstrate Business Understanding**: Show that you understand and care about project success, cost control, and schedule requirements. This credibility makes your safety requirements more acceptable.

**Be Solution-Oriented**: Instead of simply saying "no" to unsafe requests, propose alternatives that meet both safety and business needs.

**Pick Your Battles**: Focus your strongest positions on the most critical safety issues while showing flexibility on less critical matters.

**Track and Communicate Results**: Document how good safety practices contribute to project success, cost savings, and schedule reliability.

# Professional Development in Ethics

Ethical decision-making skills develop through experience, reflection, and ongoing education. Commit to continuous improvement in your ethical reasoning and professional conduct.

## Continuing Education in Ethics

**Professional Conferences**: Many safety conferences include sessions on ethics and professional responsibility. Attend these sessions regularly and participate in discussions.

**Ethics Training Programs**: Some organizations offer specialized ethics training for safety professionals. These programs provide frameworks for decision-making and case studies for practice.

**Professional Reading**: Stay current with ethics literature in safety journals and professional publications. Understanding how other professionals handle ethical dilemmas expands your own decision-making toolkit.

**Peer Discussions**: Regular conversations with other safety professionals about ethical challenges help develop your reasoning skills and provide support when facing difficult decisions.

## Building Ethical Reflection Habits

**Regular Self-Assessment**: Periodically examine your own decision-making patterns and ethical standards. Are you maintaining consistency with your stated principles?

**Seeking Feedback**: Ask trusted colleagues and mentors for their perspectives on your ethical decision-making. External viewpoints can reveal blind spots or confirm good practices.

**Learning from Mistakes**: When you make poor ethical decisions, analyze what went wrong and how you can improve. Ethical development requires honest self-examination.

**Mentoring Others**: Teaching ethical principles to junior professionals helps reinforce your own commitment and provides opportunities to think through complex situations.

# Your Ethical Legacy

Throughout your career in construction safety, you will make thousands of decisions that affect worker safety, project success, and professional standards. The cumulative impact of these decisions creates your ethical legacy - the lasting influence of your professional conduct on the people and organizations you serve.

## Questions for Reflection

As you advance in your safety career, regularly consider these fundamental questions:

- **Consistency**: Are my actions consistently aligned with my stated ethical principles?
- **Impact**: How do my decisions affect the workers whose safety I'm responsible for protecting?
- **Integrity**: Can I explain and defend my professional decisions to colleagues, family, and the public?
- **Growth**: Am I continuously improving my ability to handle ethical challenges?
- **Legacy**: What kind of safety professional do I want to be remembered as?

## Contributing to Professional Standards

**Lead by Example**: Your ethical conduct influences other safety professionals and contributes to overall professional standards in the construction industry.

**Share Knowledge**: Contribute to professional discussions about ethics through writing, speaking, and mentoring activities.

**Support Colleagues**: Help other safety professionals navigate ethical challenges by sharing your experience and providing guidance.

**Advance the Profession**: Participate in professional

organizations and activities that promote ethical standards and professional development.

The construction safety profession exists to protect workers and save lives. This fundamental mission provides clear direction for ethical decision-making: when in doubt, choose the path that best serves worker safety and human well-being. Your commitment to ethical practice not only protects your professional reputation but also upholds the trust that workers, employers, and society place in safety professionals.

Remember that ethical practice is not about perfection - it's about consistently striving to do the right thing, learning from mistakes, and maintaining your commitment to the principles that make safety work meaningful. The construction industry needs safety professionals who combine technical competence with unwavering ethical standards. Your dedication to both makes you part of the solution to construction safety challenges and contributes to a culture where every worker can expect to return home safely at the end of each day.

# APPENDICES

## Appendix A: Key OSHA Construction Standards Reference

**29 CFR 1926 - Safety and Health Regulations for Construction**

**Subpart C - General Safety and Health Provisions**
- 1926.95 - Personal protective and life saving equipment
- 1926.96 - Occupational foot protection
- 1926.100 - Head protection
- 1926.101 - Hearing protection
- 1926.102 - Eye and face protection
- 1926.103 - Respiratory protection

**Subpart D - Occupational Health and Environmental Controls**
- 1926.50 - Medical services and first aid
- 1926.51 - Sanitation
- 1926.52 - Occupational noise exposure
- 1926.53 - Ionizing radiation
- 1926.54 - Nonionizing radiation
- 1926.55 - Gases, vapors, fumes, dusts, and mists
- 1926.56 - Illumination
- 1926.57 - Ventilation
- 1926.58 - Asbestos
- 1926.59 - Hazard communication
- 1926.60 - Methylenedianiline
- 1926.61 - Retention of DOT markings, placards and labels

**Subpart E - Personal Protective and Life Saving Equipment**
- 1926.95 - Personal protective equipment
- 1926.96 - Occupational foot protection
- 1926.100 - Head protection
- 1926.101 - Hearing protection
- 1926.102 - Eye and face protection
- 1926.103 - Respiratory protection
- 1926.104 - Safety belts, lifelines, and lanyards
- 1926.105 - Safety nets
- 1926.106 - Working over or near water

**Subpart F - Fire Protection and Prevention**
- 1926.150 - Fire protection
- 1926.151 - Fire prevention
- 1926.152 - Flammable liquids
- 1926.153 - Liquefied petroleum gas (LP-Gas)
- 1926.154 - Temporary heating devices
- 1926.155 - Definitions applicable to this subpart

**Subpart G - Signs, Signals, and Barricades**
- 1926.200 - Accident prevention signs and tags
- 1926.201 - Signaling
- 1926.202 - Barricades

**Subpart H - Materials Handling, Storage, Use, and Disposal**
- 1926.250 - General requirements for storage
- 1926.251 - Rigging equipment for material handling
- 1926.252 - Disposal of waste materials

**Subpart I – Tools - Hand and Power**
- 1926.300 - General requirements
- 1926.301 - Hand tools
- 1926.302 - Power-operated hand tools
- 1926.303 - Abrasive wheels and tools
- 1926.304 - Woodworking tools
- 1926.305 – Jacks - lever and ratchet, screw, and hydraulic
- 1926.306 - Air receivers
- 1926.307 - Mechanical power-transmission apparatus

## Subpart J - Welding and Cutting
- 1926.350 - Gas welding and cutting
- 1926.351 - Arc welding and cutting
- 1926.352 - Fire prevention
- 1926.353 - Ventilation and protection in welding, cutting, and heating
- 1926.354 - Welding, cutting, and heating in way of preservative coatings

## Subpart K - Electrical
- 1926.400 - Introduction
- 1926.401 - [Reserved]
- 1926.402 - Applicability
- 1926.403 - General requirements
- 1926.404 - Wiring design and protection
- 1926.405 - Wiring methods, components, and equipment for general use
- 1926.406 - Specific purpose equipment and installations
- 1926.407 - Hazardous (classified) locations
- 1926.408 - Special systems
- 1926.416 - General requirements
- 1926.417 - Lockout and tagging of circuits

## Subpart L - Scaffolds
- 1926.450 - Scope, application and definitions applicable to this subpart
- 1926.451 - General requirements
- 1926.452 - Additional requirements applicable to specific types of scaffolds
- 1926.453 - Aerial lifts
- 1926.454 - Training requirements

## Subpart M - Fall Protection
- 1926.500 - Scope, application, and definitions applicable to this subpart
- 1926.501 - Duty to have fall protection
- 1926.502 - Fall protection systems criteria and practices
- 1926.503 - Training requirements

## Subpart N - Helicopters, Hoists, Elevators, and Conveyors
- 1926.550 - Cranes and derricks
- 1926.551 - Helicopters
- 1926.552 - Material hoists, personnel hoists, and elevators
- 1926.553 - Base-mounted drum hoists
- 1926.554 - Overhead hoists
- 1926.555 - Conveyors

## Subpart O - Motor Vehicles, Mechanized Equipment, and Marine Operations
- 1926.600 - Equipment
- 1926.601 - Motor vehicles
- 1926.602 - Material handling equipment
- 1926.603 - Pile driving equipment
- 1926.604 - Site clearing
- 1926.605 - Marine operations and equipment
- 1926.606 - Definitions applicable to this subpart

## Subpart P - Excavations
- 1926.650 - Scope, application, and definitions applicable to this subpart
- 1926.651 - Specific excavation requirements
- 1926.652 - Requirements for protective systems

## Subpart Q - Concrete and Masonry Construction
- 1926.700 - Scope, application, and definitions applicable to this subpart
- 1926.701 - General requirements
- 1926.702 - Requirements for equipment and tools
- 1926.703 - Requirements for cast-in-place concrete
- 1926.704 - Requirements for precast concrete
- 1926.705 - Requirements for lift-slab construction operations
- 1926.706 - Requirements for masonry construction

## Subpart R - Steel Erection
- 1926.750 - Scope

- 1926.751 - Definitions
- 1926.752 - Site layout, site-specific erection plan and construction sequence
- 1926.753 - Hoisting and rigging
- 1926.754 - Structural steel assembly
- 1926.755 - Column anchorage
- 1926.756 - Beams and columns
- 1926.757 - Open web steel joists
- 1926.758 - Systems-engineered metal buildings
- 1926.759 - Falling object protection
- 1926.760 - Fall protection
- 1926.761 - Training

## Subpart S - Underground Construction, Caissons, Cofferdams, and Compressed Air
- 1926.800 - Underground construction
- 1926.801 - Caissons
- 1926.802 - Cofferdams
- 1926.803 - Compressed air

## Subpart T - Demolition
- 1926.850 - Preparatory operations
- 1926.851 - Stairs, passageways, and ladders
- 1926.852 - Chutes
- 1926.853 - Removal of materials through floor openings
- 1926.854 - Removal of walls, masonry sections, and chimneys
- 1926.855 - Manual removal of floors
- 1926.856 - Removal of walls, floors, and material with equipment
- 1926.857 - Storage
- 1926.858 - Removal of steel construction
- 1926.859 - Mechanical demolition
- 1926.860 - Selective demolition by explosives

## Subpart U - Blasting and the Use of Explosives
- 1926.900 - General provisions
- 1926.901 - Blaster qualifications
- 1926.902 - Surface transportation of explosives

- 1926.903 - Underground transportation of explosives
- 1926.904 - Storage of explosives and blasting agents
- 1926.905 - Loading of explosives or blasting agents
- 1926.906 - Initiation of explosive charges - electric blasting
- 1926.907 - Use of safety fuse
- 1926.908 - Use of detonating cord
- 1926.909 - Firing the blast
- 1926.910 - Inspection after blasting
- 1926.911 - Misfires
- 1926.912 - Underwater blasting
- 1926.913 - Blasting in excavation work under compressed air
- 1926.914 - Definitions applicable to this subpart

## Subpart V - Power Transmission and Distribution
- 1926.950 - General requirements
- 1926.951 - Tools and protective equipment
- 1926.952 - Mechanical equipment
- 1926.953 - Material handling
- 1926.954 - Grounding for protection of employees
- 1926.955 - Overhead lines
- 1926.956 - Underground lines
- 1926.957 - Construction in energized substations
- 1926.958 - External load helicopters
- 1926.959 - Lineman's body belts, safety straps, and lanyards
- 1926.960 - Definitions applicable to this subpart

## Subpart W - Rollover Protective Structures; Overhead Protection
- 1926.1000 - Rollover protective structures (ROPS) for material handling equipment
- 1926.1001 - Minimum performance criteria for rollover protective structures for designated scrapers, loaders, dozers, graders, and crawler tractors
- 1926.1002 - Protective frames (roll-over protective structures, known as ROPS) for wheel-type

agricultural and industrial tractors used in construction
- 1926.1003 - Overhead protection for operators of agricultural and industrial tractors

## Subpart X - Stairways and Ladders
- 1926.1050 - Scope, application, and definitions applicable to this subpart
- 1926.1051 - General requirements
- 1926.1052 - Stairways
- 1926.1053 - Ladders
- 1926.1060 - Training requirements

# Appendix B: Professional Certification Comparison Chart

## Entry-Level Certifications

| Certification | Issuing Organization | Experience Required | Education Required | Exam Format | Validity Period | Annual Maintenance |
|---|---|---|---|---|---|---|
| Associate Safety Professional (ASP) | Board of Certified Safety Professionals (BCSP) | 1 year safety experience | Bachelor's degree (any field) | 200 multiple choice questions | Lifetime (convert to CSP within 5 years) | N/A |
| Graduate Safety Practitioner (GSP) | BCSP | None | Bachelor's in safety/occupational health OR Master's degree | 200 multiple choice questions | 5 years to convert to ASP/CSP | N/A |
| Construction Health & Safety Technician (CHST) | BCSP | 1 year construction safety experience | High school diploma + construction safety education | 200 multiple choice questions | 5 years | 30 CEUs every 5 years |
| OSHA 30-Hour Construction | OSHA Training Institute (OTI) | None | None | Training completion | Lifetime | None required |

## Advanced Certifications

| Certification | Issuing Organization | Experience Required | Education Required | Exam Format | Validity Period | Annual Maintenance |
|---|---|---|---|---|---|---|
| Certified Safety Professional (CSP) | BCSP | 4+ years safety experience | Bachelor's degree | 200 multiple choice questions | 5 years | 30 CEUs every 5 years |
| Occupational Health & Safety Technologist (OHST) | BCSP | 3+ years safety/health experience | Bachelor's in safety/health OR 5+ years experience | 200 multiple choice questions | 5 years | 30 CEUs every 5 years |
| Safety Management Specialist (SMS) | BCSP | 8+ years management experience | Bachelor's degree + CSP certification | 150 multiple choice questions | 5 years | 30 CEUs every 5 years |
| Certified Industrial Hygienist (CIH) | American Board of Industrial Hygiene (ABIH) | 4+ years IH experience | Bachelor's in physical/biological science | 195 multiple choice questions | 5 years | 32 CEUs every 4 years |

## Specialized Certifications

| Certification | Issuing Organization | Focus Area | Experience Required | Exam Format | Validity Period |
|---|---|---|---|---|---|
| Certified Crane Operator | National Commission for Certification of Crane Operators (NCCCO) | Crane Operations | Varies by crane type | Written + practical | 5 years |
| Certified Fire Protection Specialist (CFPS) | National Association of Fire Protection Engineers (NFPE) | Fire Protection Engineering | 4+ years experience | Multiple choice + essay | 3 years |
| Certified Environmental, Safety & Health Trainer (CET) | Institute of Hazardous Materials Management (IHMM) | Training & Education | 2+ years training experience | 150 multiple choice questions | 5 years |
| Certified Hazardous Materials Manager (CHMM) | IHMM | Hazardous Materials | 3+ years hazmat experience | 150 multiple choice questions | 5 years |
| Professional Engineer (PE) | State Licensing Boards | Various Engineering Disciplines | 4+ years engineering experience | State-specific format | Varies by state |

## OSHA Training Certifications

| Program | Duration | Target Audience | Certification Level | Validity |
|---|---|---|---|---|
| OSHA 10-Hour Construction | 10 hours | Entry-level workers | Certificate of completion | Lifetime |
| OSHA 30-Hour Construction | 30 hours | Supervisors, safety personnel | Certificate of completion | Lifetime |
| OSHA 500 - Trainer Course | 40 hours | Prospective OSHA trainers | Authorization to teach OSHA 10/30 | 4 years |
| OSHA 501 - Trainer Update | 8 hours | Current OSHA trainers | Maintains trainer authorization | Required every 4 years |
| OSHA 510 - Standards for Construction | 32 hours | Safety professionals | Certificate of completion | Lifetime |
| OSHA 511 - Standards for General Industry | 32 hours | Safety professionals | Certificate of completion | Lifetime |

## Certification Investment Analysis

### Cost Comparison (Approximate 2024 Fees):
- ASP/GSP: $350-$450
- CSP: $450-$550
- CHST: $350-$450
- OHST: $350-$450
- CIH: $1,200-$1,500
- OSHA 30-Hour: $150-$300
- OSHA 500: $1,500-$2,500

### Return on Investment Considerations:
- Entry-level certifications: 5-15% salary increase
- Professional certifications (CSP, CIH): 15-25% salary increase
- Specialized certifications: Variable based on market demand
- Management certifications: 20-30% salary increase potential

### Career Progression Recommendations:
1. **New Graduates**: Start with GSP, convert to ASP/CSP
2. **Experienced Professionals**: Target CSP as primary credential

3. **Construction Focus**: CHST + OSHA certifications
4. **Management Track**: CSP → SMS progression
5. **Technical Specialization**: Add specialized certifications to base CSP

# Appendix C: Sample Forms and Checklists

## C.1 Daily Safety Inspection Checklist

**Project Information:**
- Project Name: _____
- Date: _____
- Weather Conditions: _____
- Inspector: _____
- Signature: _____

**Personal Protective Equipment**
- [ ] Hard hats worn by all personnel
- [ ] Safety glasses/goggles in use where required
- [ ] High-visibility vests worn in designated areas
- [ ] Safety footwear appropriate for conditions
- [ ] Hearing protection used in noise areas
- [ ] Respiratory protection when required
- [ ] PPE in good condition and properly maintained

**Fall Protection**
- [ ] Guardrails installed where required (6 feet or higher)
- [ ] Personal fall arrest systems inspected and properly used
- [ ] Safety nets installed where applicable
- [ ] Hole covers in place and properly secured
- [ ] Ladder safety practices observed
- [ ] Scaffold systems properly erected and tagged
- [ ] Fall protection training current for exposed workers

**Housekeeping**
- [ ] Work areas clean and free of debris
- [ ] Materials properly stored and secured

- [ ] Walking/working surfaces clear of hazards
- [ ] Trash containers available and used
- [ ] Spill cleanup materials available
- [ ] Emergency egress routes clear

**Electrical Safety**
- [ ] Temporary electrical installations properly protected
- [ ] GFCI protection in place for wet/damp locations
- [ ] Electrical cords in good condition
- [ ] Proper grounding of equipment
- [ ] Electrical panels accessible and labeled
- [ ] Lockout/tagout procedures followed

**Tools and Equipment**
- [ ] Power tools inspected before use
- [ ] Guards in place on power tools
- [ ] Proper tool selection for tasks
- [ ] Tools stored properly when not in use
- [ ] Extension cords appropriate for application
- [ ] Equipment operators properly trained/certified

**Fire Prevention**
- [ ] Hot work permits obtained where required
- [ ] Fire extinguishers available and accessible
- [ ] Flammable materials properly stored
- [ ] Smoking restrictions observed
- [ ] Emergency evacuation routes posted and clear

**Excavation/Trenching**
- [ ] Excavations properly sloped or shored
- [ ] Ladders provided for egress (25 feet or closer)
- [ ] Spoil piles setback appropriately
- [ ] Utilities located before digging
- [ ] Competent person inspection completed
- [ ] Atmospheric testing conducted if required

**Comments/Corrective Actions Needed:**

**Follow-up Required:** [ ] Yes [ ] No **Date for Re-inspection:** _____

## C.2 Job Hazard Analysis (JHA) Template
**Job/Task:** _____
**Location:** _____ **Date:** _____
_____ **Prepared by:** _____
_____ **Reviewed by:** _____

**Personnel Required:**
- Number of workers: ____
- Required certifications: _____
- Special training needed: _____

**Tools/Equipment Required:**

**Materials Required:**

**Personal Protective Equipment Required:**
- [ ] Hard hat
- [ ] Safety glasses/goggles
- [ ] Hearing protection
- [ ] Respiratory protection
- [ ] Hand protection
- [ ] Foot protection
- [ ] Fall protection
- [ ] High-visibility clothing
- [ ] Other: _____

**Environmental Conditions:**
- Weather considerations: _____
- Noise levels: _____
- Chemical exposures: _____
- Physical hazards: _____

| Step | Task Description | Potential Hazards | Controls/Safe Procedures |
|------|------------------|-------------------|--------------------------|

1

2

3

4

5

6

7

8

**Emergency Procedures:**
- Emergency contact: _____
- Nearest hospital: _____
- Emergency assembly point: _____
- Special emergency equipment: _____

**Training Requirements:**
- General safety orientation: [ ] Required
- Task-specific training: [ ] Required
- Equipment operation training: [ ] Required
- Emergency response training: [ ] Required

**Approval:**
- Supervisor: _____ Date: _____
- Safety Manager: _____ Date: _____
- Project Manager: _____ Date: _____

## C.3 Incident Investigation Report Template
**CONFIDENTIAL - INCIDENT INVESTIGATION REPORT**

**Incident Information:**
- Report Number: _____
- Date of Incident: _____
- Time of Incident: _____
- Location: _____
- Project/Site: _____

**Injured Person(s):**
- Name: _____
- Job Title: _____
- Department: _____

- Supervisor: _____
- Years of Experience: _____
- Date of Hire: _____

**Incident Classification:**
- [ ] Near Miss
- [ ] First Aid
- [ ] Medical Treatment
- [ ] Restricted Work
- [ ] Lost Time Injury
- [ ] Fatality
- [ ] Property Damage Only

**Incident Description:** (Describe what happened, including sequence of events)

_____
_____
_____

**Immediate Cause(s):**
- [ ] Unsafe act
- [ ] Unsafe condition
- [ ] Equipment failure
- [ ] Environmental factor
- [ ] Other: _____

**Root Cause Analysis: Why did this incident occur?**

_____

Why? _____
2. Why? _____
3. Why? _____
4. Why? _____
5. Why? _____

**Contributing Factors:**
- [ ] Inadequate training
- [ ] Insufficient supervision
- [ ] Improper work procedures
- [ ] Defective equipment
- [ ] Poor housekeeping
- [ ] Inadequate PPE
- [ ] Communication failure
- [ ] Time pressure
- [ ] Other: _____

**Witnesses:**
    1. Name: _____ Contact: _____

    2. Name: _____ Contact: _____

    3. Name: _____ Contact: _____

**Photos Taken:** [ ] Yes [ ] No **Evidence Collected:** [ ] Yes [ ] No
**Measurements Taken:** [ ] Yes [ ] No
**Corrective Actions:**

  Action Item    Responsible Person    Target Date    Completion Date




**Investigation Team:**
- Lead Investigator: _____
- Team Members: _____

**Report Completed by:** _____
**Date:** _____ **Signature:** _____

## C.4 Safety Meeting Documentation Form
**Safety Meeting Record**
**Meeting Information:**
- Date: _____
- Time: _____ to _____
- Location: _____
- Meeting Leader: _____
- Project/Department: _____

**Topics Discussed:**
- [ ] Recent incidents/near misses
- [ ] New safety procedures
- [ ] PPE requirements
- [ ] Hazard recognition
- [ ] Emergency procedures
- [ ] Training updates

- [ ] Regulatory changes
- [ ] Seasonal safety topics
- [ ] Other: _____

**Main Discussion Points:**

_____
_____
_____

**Safety Concerns Raised:**

_____
_____
_____

**Action Items:**

Item    Responsible Person    Due Date


**Attendees:**

Name (Print)    Department    Signature


**Materials Distributed:**
- [ ] Safety bulletins
- [ ] Procedure updates
- [ ] Training materials
- [ ] Reference guides
- [ ] Other: _____

**Next Meeting Scheduled:** _____
**Meeting Leader Signature:** _____

## C.5 Permit-to-Work Template
### HOT WORK PERMIT
**Permit Information:**
- Permit Number: _____
- Date Issued: _____
- Valid From: _____ To: _____
- Location: _____
- Building/Area: _____

**Work Description:**
_____
_____

**Equipment to be Used:**
- [ ] Welding equipment
- [ ] Cutting torch
- [ ] Grinder
- [ ] Soldering equipment
- [ ] Other: _____

**Pre-Work Requirements Completed:**
- [ ] Fire watch assigned and trained
- [ ] Combustible materials removed (35-foot radius)
- [ ] Fire extinguishers available
- [ ] Emergency procedures reviewed
- [ ] Work area ventilation adequate
- [ ] Personal protective equipment available
- [ ] Hot work procedures reviewed with crew

**Atmospheric Testing (if required):**
- Oxygen: ____% (19.5-23.5% required)
- Lower Explosive Limit: ____% (must be <10%)
- Toxic Gases: ____ppm
- Tested by: _____
- Time: _____

**Personnel:**
- Person Performing Work: _____
- Fire Watch: _____
- Supervisor: _____

**Authorizations:**
- Requested by: _____ Date: _____
- Supervisor Approval: _____ Date: _____

- Safety Approval: _____ Date: _____
- Fire Marshal (if required): _____ Date: _____

**Fire Watch Certification:** "I understand my duties as fire watch and will maintain continuous surveillance of the work area during hot work operations and for 30 minutes after completion."

Fire Watch Signature: _____

**Work Completion:**
- Work Completed: Time: _____ Date: _____
- Fire Watch Maintained 30 minutes after completion: [ ] Yes
- Area inspected for fire hazards: [ ] Yes
- Permit closed by: _____

# Appendix D: Recommended Reading and Resources

## Essential Books for Construction Safety Professionals

**Foundational Texts:**

1. **"Construction Safety Management and Engineering" by Charles Trethewy and Grant Mills**
   - Comprehensive overview of safety management systems
   - Practical guidance for implementing safety programs
   - Case studies from international construction projects
2. **"Construction Safety Handbook" by V. J. Davies and K. Tomasin**
   - Detailed coverage of OSHA construction standards
   - Practical checklists and forms
   - Risk assessment methodologies
3. **"Accident/Incident Prevention Techniques" by Dan Petersen**
   - Classic text on safety management

- principles
- Behavioral safety concepts
- Accident causation theories
4. **"Managing Construction Safety and Health" by Charles Levitt and Nancy Samelson**
    - Systems approach to construction safety
    - Legal compliance requirements
    - Program development strategies

**Specialized Topics:**

5. **"Fall Protection: Systems and Applications" by Steven Hays**
    - Comprehensive guide to fall protection systems
    - Equipment selection and inspection
    - Training program development
6. **"Crane Safety: Mobile Cranes, Tower Cranes, Overhead Cranes" by Lawrence Shapiro**
    - Equipment-specific safety requirements
    - Operator training principles
    - Inspection and maintenance procedures
7. **"Excavation & Trenching Operations" by Jeffrey Lew**
    - Soil classification and analysis
    - Protective system design
    - OSHA compliance requirements
8. **"Industrial Fire Protection Engineering" by Robert Benedetti**
    - Fire prevention in construction
    - Emergency response planning
    - Code compliance strategies

**Leadership and Management:**

9. **"The Safety Gurus: Lessons in Safety Leadership" by Mike Williamsen**
    - Leadership principles for safety

- professionals
  - Influence strategies
  - Organizational change management
10. **"Creating a Safety Culture" by Rob Long**
    - Safety culture development
    - Behavioral change strategies
    - Measurement and assessment

## Professional Journals and Publications
### Primary Professional Journals:
- **Professional Safety** (American Society of Safety Professionals)
  - Monthly publication with peer-reviewed articles
  - Case studies and best practices
  - Technical updates and regulatory changes
- **Safety and Health** (National Safety Council)
  - Practical articles for safety practitioners
  - Industry trends and innovations
  - Training and development resources
- **Construction Executive** (Associated Builders and Contractors)
  - Business and safety integration
  - Industry leadership perspectives
  - Technology and innovation coverage
- **ENR (Engineering News-Record)**
  - Construction industry news and trends
  - Safety performance benchmarks
  - Major project case studies

### Specialized Publications:
- **Occupational Hazards** - Workplace safety across industries
- **Industrial Safety & Hygiene News** - Technical and regulatory updates
- **Safety+Health Magazine** - National Safety Council publication
- **ASSE Professional Development Conference Proceedings** - Annual collection of technical papers

## Online Resources and Websites
### Government Resources:
- **OSHA.gov** - Occupational Safety and Health Administration
  - Complete construction standards (29 CFR 1926)
  - Compliance assistance tools
  - Training materials and guidance documents
- **CDC.gov/NIOSH** - National Institute for Occupational Safety and Health
  - Research publications and criteria documents
  - Health hazard evaluations
  - Technology transfer materials
- **MSHA.gov** - Mine Safety and Health Administration
  - Standards for construction in mining environments
  - Training materials and resources

### Professional Organizations:
- **ASSP.org** - American Society of Safety Professionals
  - Professional development resources
  - Networking opportunities
  - Certification information
- **BCSP.org** - Board of Certified Safety Professionals
  - Certification requirements and processes
  - Continuing education opportunities
  - Professional standards
- **NSC.org** - National Safety Council
  - Statistical resources and trend analysis
  - Training programs and materials
  - Safety culture resources

### Industry Organizations:
- **AGC.org** - Associated General Contractors of America
  - Safety programs and resources
  - Best practices sharing
  - Training and certification programs
- **ABC.org** - Associated Builders and Contractors
  - STEP (Safety Training Evaluation Process)

program
  - Safety performance benchmarking
  - Training resources

## Technology and Software Resources
**Safety Management Software:**
- **iAuditor** - Mobile inspection and audit platform
- **SafetyCulture** - Incident reporting and communication
- **Procore** - Construction project management with safety modules
- **PlanGrid** - Field collaboration with safety documentation

**Training and Communication Tools:**
- **Adobe Captivate** - E-learning development
- **Articulate Storyline** - Interactive training content
- **Zoom/Teams** - Virtual training delivery
- **Yammer/Slack** - Safety communication platforms

**Data Analysis and Reporting:**
- **Microsoft Power BI** - Safety metrics dashboard
- **Tableau** - Data visualization and analysis
- **Excel** - Basic statistical analysis and reporting
- **R/Python** - Advanced statistical analysis

## Continuing Education Opportunities
**University Programs:**
- **Murray State University** - Occupational Safety and Health (M.S.)
- **Central Missouri State University** - Industrial Safety (M.S.)
- **Indiana University of Pennsylvania** - Safety Sciences (M.S.)
- **University of Alabama at Birmingham** - Occupational Health and Safety (M.P.H.)
- **Montana Tech** - Industrial Safety and Health (M.S.)

**Professional Development Providers:**
- **American Society of Safety Professionals** - Seminars and webinars
- **National Safety Council** - Professional development courses
- **Board of Certified Safety Professionals** - Continuing education programs
- **Construction Industry Institute** - Research-based education

**Online Learning Platforms:**
- **Coursera** - University-level safety courses
- **edX** - Professional certificate programs
- **LinkedIn Learning** - Skill-specific training modules
- **Udemy** - Practical safety management courses

## Emergency Response and Medical Resources
**Emergency Response Training:**
- **American Red Cross** - First aid and CPR certification
- **American Heart Association** - CPR and AED training
- **National Safety Council** - First aid and emergency response

## Disclaimer
The information provided in Construction Safety: Your Complete Guide to Starting a Career in Safety is for educational and informational purposes only. While every effort has been made to ensure the accuracy and completeness of the content, the author and publisher make no representations or warranties of any kind, express or implied, about the reliability, suitability, or applicability of the procedures, guidelines, or recommendations contained herein.

**Safety First:**

This book is not a substitute for professional training, OSHA certification, or site-specific safety protocols. Always follow your employer's policies and local, state, and federal regulations.

Construction hazards vary by project, environment, and jurisdiction. Readers must assess risks and implement controls appropriate to their unique circumstances.

The author and publisher disclaim any liability for injuries, losses, or damages resulting from the use or misuse of this book's content.

**Regulatory Compliance:**
Laws and standards (including OSHA regulations) may change over time. For official OSHA standards and updates, visit www.osha.gov.

Case studies and examples are illustrative only and do not constitute legal or safety advice.

**Trademarks & Rights:**
All product names, logos, and brands mentioned are the property of their respective owners.

**Important Note:**
The author is not responsible for reader interpretation or application of this material. By reading this book, you acknowledge and accept full responsibility for your safety decisions and actions. When in doubt, consult a qualified safety professional.

www.ingramcontent.com/pod-product-compliance
Lightning Source LLC
LaVergne TN
LVHW020109100426
835512LV00041B/3207